Also by Kenneth Kaye

The Mental and Social Life of Babies
Family Rules
Workplace Wars
The Dynamics of Family Business
Birds of Evanston (stories)

Trust Me

Helping Our Young Adults Financially

Kenneth Kaye, Ph.D.
with Nick Kaye

iUniverse, Inc.
New York Bloomington

Trust Me
Helping Our Young Adults Financially

iUniverse books may be ordered through booksellers or by contacting:

iUniverse
1663 Liberty Drive
Bloomington, IN 47403
www.iuniverse.com
1-800-Authors (1-800-288-4677)

ISBN: 978-1-4401-1977-4 (pbk)
ISBN: 978-1-4401-1979-8 (cloth)
ISBN: 978-1-4401-1978-1 (ebk)

Printed in the United States of America

iUniverse rev. date: 3/27/2009

To the memory of Saul and Juanita Kaye

Contents

Acknowledgments

Nick and I thank his older brother, Lev, for the suggestion to write this book, and their youngest sister, Hope, for going over the whole manuscript (some chapters twice) with an astute red pencil.

I thank my colleague and friend, Sara Hamilton, for reviewing and contributing to Chapter XIII, and for many conversations about our clients' efforts (some successful, some not) to prepare their children for inherited wealth.

Profound thanks go to the many clients themselves, as well as colleagues and friends who shared their experiences with me over the years.

Finally, to my co-author and best teacher on this subject, a model of persistence when life gets tough: for your amazing creativity, energy, and passion to improve whatever situation you find yourself in, and for your loving friendship, thank you, son.

— K.K.

My parent's patience gave me the breathing room to learn from experience and find my own good judgment. I have been wonderfully fortunate in my sisters, brother, and friends, all of whom enrich my life irrespective of money. As I pat myself on the back for growing up, I hope this book brings similar satisfaction to others.

—N.K.

I. "Trust Me"

> *In the period after adolescence, as young people go out to make their way in the world, relationships between the generations normally become easier and on a more equal plane—except when the would-be adults fall into the worrisome condition of requiring parental support without meeting parental expectations.*
>
> *Good news: We don't have to grit our teeth and shut our mouths as our sons and daughters sink into financial trouble. The solution is to give young people the tools they need to earn our trust. At the same time, we earn their trust by proving to be mentors who genuinely respect their independence.*

"Trust me," my younger son said. He said it with conviction. Nick's intentions were generally good. He sincerely believed he would prove trustworthy. Yet his dreams were unrealistic: so many times, from his early teens into his twenties, he disappointed himself as well as his parents. The amplifiers, speakers, and turntables that were sure to pay for themselves many times over in deejay jobs, didn't. The laptop continued west on a Greyhound bus, never to return, when he dawdled at a rest stop. Naturally, we advanced the funds for a replacement. (Notwithstanding both parents' degrees in developmental psychology and my decades as a family counselor and author of titles like *Raising Responsible Children*.) There were countless mishaps, tickets, and related expenses all three of us would prefer to forget. The freelance web design work that was going to earn him, for example, $750 for ten hours' work turned out to take him sixty hours, and weeks more before the clients finally paid. Then there were the ones who never paid. His optimistic rent check, mailed to a landlord in expectation of being able to beat it to the bank with a promised payment from a client, bounced. Cell phone and Internet were cancelled at various times for nonpayment, leaving him cut off from his livelihood unless his mother or I hastily rescued him. Time and again, we found reasons to keep the wolf from his door—sometimes enforcing conditions, sometimes not. Our son's "trust me" assurance had long since acquired the opposite meaning to us: a red flag.

Yet we wanted to trust Nick, every bit as much as he wanted to earn our trust. The hopes of parents and youth are basically the same: both want the younger generation to grow up. We want them to be independent, yet safe; so do they. We're more concerned about their happiness than about their long term financial security; so are they. We parents worry more about a variety of mishaps than about how much money they have in the bank. When I helped my daughter buy her first car, my concern wasn't the money, it was her safety on the road. When Nick asked me to come to his rescue with yet another small loan, I wasn't worried about whether I'd get those few hundred dollars back. What I worried about was that latest setback in his struggle to become responsible.

How do we constructively deal with those worries, as our children leave home and we're less and less in touch with their lives? Here's the good news: both generations now begin to repair the estrangement of adolescence. We've reached the stage (at last!) of rapprochement, testing the possibilities of coming together on a more equal footing.

We parents tend to cope in two contradictory ways with our anxiety about letting go. One thing we do—it seems to be instinctive, unfortunately—is to patronize them with bossy, judgmental, unwelcome advice. Our attempts to protect them from the possible consequences of immature behavior threaten to smother them.

But at other times we go the opposite way, into denial. We set our worries aside, avoid asking questions, suppress our doubts about the path they seem to be on, and tell ourselves they'll figure it out if we don't make ourselves crazy. Unfortunately, deep down we know there's a thin line between letting children learn from experience and letting them drown.

So, is it a choice between smothering them with protection or waiting for experience to drown them? Happily, there's a third alternative: balancing *welcome* supervision with *usable* experience. Thus we grow beyond our relationship with a dependent child into one between two somewhat independent adults. When we succeed, we've moved the relationship from a dominating one to a kind of parity:

There's no more satisfying (though perhaps wistful) moment in parenthood than the realization that our children are truly adults. How do we get to that moment? It happens by trust being earned on *both* sides. We had their complete trust when they were little children, but as adolescents they had to test whether we'd really let them be separate individuals, making their own choices. They had reason to doubt that we'd ever accept their independence. Now, as they come out of adolescence and earn our trust by showing responsibility, we can re-earn *their* trust by sincerely treating them like adults.

---

by Nick Kaye:

From adolescence through my early twenties, I've been fighting the law. The law of supply and demand, that is: the world's demand for a steady supply of my money. It doesn't take a Ph.D. to realize the law will get you in the end.

My turbulent journey wasn't such a catastrophe as Dad enjoys painting it. For example, those amps, speakers, turntables, synthesizers and samplers didn't "pay for themselves" by his measure, but I grew up creating music. I'm proud of my creative successes and fantastic unconventional friends. Who knows why my learning to become financially responsible required more discipline and effort,

3

on Dad's part as well as mine, than my three "normal" siblings did? Happily, our efforts have paid off in a mutually appreciative father-son relationship.

Since we see many things differently, I'll insert my own perspective throughout the book in this typeface.

Why focus on money?

This book deals with one part of the growth into responsible independence: how the young person learns to acquire, spend, save, and handle money, including earnings, allowances, bank accounts, bills, taxes, loans, and eventually (this should be last of all) credit cards. Do I focus on money because we parents are really obsessed with our youths' financial responsibility? Not at all. We care more about their safety, their physical and mental health, their happiness in relationships, ability to work with others, opportunities to develop their talents and pursue their dreams. Which may be why we've paid too little attention to their economic skills.

Fortunately, as they go out into the world, *the economic arena is where twenty-somethings are most open to learning from their parents*, where they're most likely to trust the parents' good intentions, and where the parents still have powerful leverage.

If all your children were cautious types who'd rather save than spend, and who asked for your sage advice and parental consent before taking each step toward independence, you'd never need this book. Nor would you need to subscribe to the website Nick and I created, www.EarnTrust.net (although the site's free tutorial material and quizzes might interest even your prudent son or daughter).

This book offers help to those with one or more offspring who haven't been so careful. Perhaps your son is endlessly creative, like Nick, whose high school grades were all A's and D's because, in classes that excited him, he was a hard working, imaginative and charming participant, while in classes that bored him he

---

A business analogy: the turnaround manager

When a business is in such bad shape that it's in danger of defaulting on its loans, its bank will typically make a deal with the owners. It extends their credit so they can continue operating, in order to turn things around—but only if they put themselves under the oversight of an expert in the field called "turnaround management."

That's what I'm going to show you how to do with the young person whose financial survival you're worried about. You might continue partially supporting them, but you'll become their consultant/mentor as well, or hire someone to act in that role.

---

would blow off assignments that determined half his grade. Or perhaps your daughter, as a child, always pushed your limits (and won, if getting money out of you was the game). Or your son had a short attention span, a reading problem, or a belief that he was "no good at math."

Yours may be the kid who had an easy time in school, breezed through early adolescence without any apparent problems, then got carried away partying with richer friends. We won't speculate about her addiction: whether it's clothes shopping, or marijuana, or traveling. Whatever the cause, it led her to *ignore or deny the facts* about her present and future circumstances. Let's cure that denial with a gentle but firm dose of reality.

Four stages

What age range is this book about? It can't be defined by years, because economic maturation varies so much across individuals. We can, however, distinguish four stages according to the changing role of money in relationships between parents and youth.

Early Teens often receive an allowance, as well as gifts and informal income from lawn work or babysitting. Although they may put some of those dollars in a savings account, much if not all of it is theirs to spend. At that stage, parents or guardians provide all the necessities and have little leverage over how teens spend their own money. This book starts when the teen stage ends, usually around the end of high school.

Dependent Youth (the first stage we'll deal with) are just beginning to learn about planned expenditures and budgets. Although not responsible for the majority of their living expenses, they do have some financial responsibilities. A parent or other mentor has begun coaching them in managing a checking account, paying certain monthly bills, and perhaps using a debit card.

Semi-independent Young Adults have definite responsibilities for a large part of their support. They live away from their parents and pay for their rent, utilities, food, and personal expenses. Their responsibilities include forwarding any bills the parent is still taking care of; as well as financial records that will be needed for insurance reimbursement or for tax filing. They take care of their own living quarters and material assets: car, electronics, clothing, and so forth. They understand and fulfill terms of any loans.

Grown-ups are what we want them to become. They may still be paying off loans, but their subsistence no longer depends on infusions from parents or anyone else. If they use credit cards, they'll do so only for payment convenience, not as continuous consumer debt. If they're among the fortunate few who can draw on a trust or other source of inherited wealth, they will live within its guidelines. Absent a trust fund, they'll earn income sufficient to support their lifestyle, including insurance premiums and health care. They'll keep documentation of income and deductible expenses, and make tax payments as required. They will seek advice rather than let a problem become an emergency.

This book is about the second and third of those stages—dependent youth and semi-independent young adults—whether they're eighteen, or twenty-eight, or already in their thirties yet not financially mature.

> ### *Young, fabulous, and broke in a nineteenth century novel*
>
> "The implicit confidence that her destiny must be one of luxurious ease, where any trouble that occurred would be well clad and provided for, had been stronger in her own mind than in her mamma's, being fed by her youthful blood and that sense of superior claims which made a large part of her consciousness. It was difficult for her to believe suddenly that her position had become one of poverty and humiliating dependence."
>
> —George Eliot, *Daniel Deronda*, 1876.

"Young, Fabulous & Broke"

Suze Orman aptly addressed my son, Nick, in her title: the *Money Book for the Young, Fabulous & Broke*. It's a phenomenon that's more universal than just our contemporary society. We can find prodigal youth in Shakespeare's plays and ancient literature (Eastern as well as Western), all the way back to the Bible.

Still, this had become a crisis in twenty-first century America even before the crisis spread to all age groups. It was already a crisis because post-adolescence had become a whole new stage in life, described by psychologist Jeffrey Arnett as "the winding road from the late teens through the twenties."[1] Social maturation now takes place six to eight years later, by one estimate, than it did a generation ago. The other reason is that youth now finish their education deeply in debt, entering an economy that is saddled with a higher percentage of debt than at any time since the 1940s.

It was a personal crisis lasting about seven years for Nick and his mother and me, but we knew we weren't alone as we heard similar woes from friends, relatives, and my clients. Do you recognize one of these young people?

---

1   Jeffrey J. Arnett, *Emerging Adulthood*. Oxford University Press, 2004.

Sheryl took a job as assistant stage manager in a small theatre company, "starting at the bottom" to pursue her dream. She has a day job, too: as a waitress in a busy downtown restaurant. She shared an apartment with two other young women, but when one of those moved out, Sheryl's share of rent and utilities suddenly grew by 50 percent. She started living off her credit card, then got a second one; and now her mother overhears her tell a friend "I have to get a third card." The annual rates Sheryl is paying on those cards, Mom learns, are both over 19 percent, plus penalties in months when she can't pay the minimums. Sheryl's parents are frankly losing faith in her fabulous future on the stage; but they do know she's definitely broke.

José had mixed success in high school. He got into a four-year college on the strength of his fabulous record on the wrestling team, decent SAT scores and recommendations from his favorite teachers. But the college's required courses and obligatory assignments didn't agree with him. He moved up two weight divisions, where he lost most of his matches. After three semesters with poor grades and some incompletes, José didn't go back. In the year since then, he's had four different jobs that "didn't work out" for one reason or another.

Dawn is a good student in a first-rate liberal arts college. She worked at Starbucks one summer, then part time throughout her junior year. The next summer, she took two courses in Spain and traveled through Europe for a month. Her "fabulous" credentials include her personality, pretty good Spanish, talents in dance and skiing, her social conscience and compassion for those less fortunate. Although she majored in comparative literature, Dawn tells her parents she'd like to pursue a career working for an international aid agency of some kind, perhaps one of the church-connected ones her family supports. Upon graduation, however, she says she's "not ready for the nine to five grind. I want to see more of the world before I settle down. And then I might want to go to grad school in something."

That's Dawn's fabulous side; what about the other side? Is she broke? Not at first glance, because she has a little money in her bank account. Since her parents have covered room and board while she's been in college, and funded her travels as extensions of the overseas courses, and she charges some of her wardrobe to Mom's credit card (with permission), and uses a family car when she's in town, the occasional part time job plus gifts from her grandmother and selling some of the clothes she doesn't plan to wear again are sufficient sources of income to maintain Dawn in her accustomed lifestyle. Ostensibly, she's thinking about how to support a year in Spain by "waitressing or being a tour guide or something." And why not? That might be an excellent idea, more sensible than going to graduate school in some field she's not really sure she'll want to pursue. What troubles her father, though, is his suspicion that Dawn hopes he'll ante up for the year in Europe as he has done for everything in her life thus far. She has hinted that she'd get more out of the proposed year of "seeing the world" if she didn't have to work. But her parents feel they footed the bill for enough of that kind of travel. On the other hand, they don't want to shut the faucet off abruptly or unreasonably.

Dawn *is* broke, in the sense that she's never lived off her own income, or even close to it. If she had a generous trust fund, then no problem: its income might sustain Dawn's travel plans. But there is no trust fund, and Dad thinks the free ride should stop after four years of higher education. He has said so, categorically. Yet Dawn's parents are well off, they could afford to subsidize a few more years, and their daughter is so fabulous, they don't want to rush her.

Matt's fabulous credentials include his talent as a guitarist and his dark, movie-star features. He plays in two bands, one of which has gigs almost every week. He lives "within his means" by not having to pay rent. His girlfriend, Monica, takes care of that, thanks to her full time job as a tattooist. (She did his back and both arms for free, too.) At twenty-eight, it's been a couple of years since Matt last asked his parents for money. They've written off, and imagine he's forgotten, the $3,000 they "loaned" him to move back to Chicago from L.A. What they can't adjust to is this thirty-five-year-old woman, Monica.

9

They could almost ignore the scary pictures on her arms and neck, but they can't help feeling she enables Matt's unrealistic view of himself as having an adult life. In fact, let's be blunt: they think Monica is trying to rope Matt into something he's nowhere near ready for. She'll press for marriage, maybe get pregnant. They assume Matt's told her that he expects to inherit some money at thirty. This is true, but not enough to support him for life, much less support a family. Although the parents' house is far from the largest or grandest one in their neighborhood, Monica doesn't hide how impressed she is by it. She's made no secret of her own family's poverty.

Matt's parents are worrying about the wrong thing, imagining that Monica is the problem. His problem, like those of Dawn, José, and Sheryl, is *his own slowness to face a realistic picture of his future* based on his actual behavior, income, and total costs of living—including those costs paid by others.

Every family's scenarios of unrealistic young adulthood are distinct in their details. What they share, I suggest, is that no matter how well those parents met the challenges of parenthood when they were putting food on the table, clothes on the backs, and a roof over the heads of their children, these young people are stumbling in the stages between Dependent and Grown-up. They're ostensibly but not actually, not sufficiently, supporting themselves. They may be earning, like Sheryl, but they're not managing the costs of living. Or they're living on almost nothing, like Matt, but getting no closer to adulthood.

As this continues year after year, it prevents the relationship between parent and child from developing beyond the adolescent stage.

Get real about where you're heading

As I pointed out in my book *Family Rules*, parenthood is essentially a paradox. Raising children is about protecting them while letting them go. We bring them into the world twice: first when we give birth to them after nine months' gestation, then again when we launch them into their own apartments after twenty or so years in the family womb. With all respect for pregnancy, let's face it: those nine months are a piece of cake compared with the twenty (or thirty) years before the real launch.

Here is the solution for young people who are out in the world but not yet in command of the skills and habits they'll need: *you, as a parent, before cutting the financial umbilical cord, need to bring home the reality of where their assumptions, denial, and inattentiveness are leading them.*

You need to simplify the tasks and teach money skills one step at a time, so the details of earning, banking, paying bills, keeping records and forecasting won't seem so overwhelming. How can you do that when they've grown up (supposedly) and moved out? At this stage, the best answer often is: the power of the purse! While still propping them up financially in one way or another, you *can* hold your son or daughter accountable by being absolutely clear (this means in writing) about what you don't subsidize and what you will subsidize *under certain conditions.* Then, follow through on those conditions. When you make a decision to bail them out of a tight spot, it's totally appropriate to place conditions on doing so. This is a wake-up call, a valuable opportunity for both of you to mend your ways. Make sure it's reflected in your Deal.

II. What's the Deal?

The first step is to be absolutely clear about what we're willing to do for our young adult children. They need money, often in the form of a loan. And they need coaching. Under what conditions can they count on getting those from you? For how long? And what's the shared goal? Your Deal describes a temporary step on the way toward responsible adulthood. Discuss it explicitly, negotiate and write out the terms, and formally sign it.

You already have a deal with each of your dependent and semi-independent children. We all do. But if it's not the clear, written, enforceable kind of Deal-with-a-capital-D, you may have been enabling the very things you're worried about.

Sheryl's parents in Chapter I enabled her credit card problem when they co-signed the lease on an apartment she couldn't afford. Matt's parents enabled his illusion that he was supporting himself with his music, when they wrote off the $3,000 he had "borrowed" from them. And Dawn's father is asking himself whether funding a year of aimless travel would be enriching her education, or enabling unrealistic assumptions about her resources.

There's nothing wrong with subsidizing a young person, whether by paying their rent, funding a clothes budget, taking over a credit card debt on more manageable terms, or letting them move back home. If it's working for both of you, don't fix it. But if you picked up this book because you're frustrated, or you fear you've let that son or daughter manipulate you, or you hear yourself nagging and nothing changes, or you suspect you're enabling a situation that isn't good for them, then you absolutely need to examine your Deal, fine-tune and clarify it.

My job is only to show you a system for making and enforcing your Deal about money—not to tell you what your Deal should be.

Clear, written, and enforceable

Carlo is a full time apprentice carpenter, working toward his journeyman certificate. He rents a studio apartment and covers all his current living expenses. Over the previous year, however, he ran up a balance of nearly $6,000 on a high interest credit card. His parents generously offer to pay that off and allow him to pay them back at a very low interest rate, with no regularly required payments. In fact, they won't expect him to begin repaying the loan for at least two years. They set four conditions: Carlo will use only a debit card; he won't borrow from any other source; he'll take a couple of online tutorials; and he'll welcome his father's mentoring and supervision of his bill paying. The Deal specifies that those conditions continue until Carlo meets certain criteria including a positive cash flow and no bank penalties or late fees for a year. Finally, it spells out the goal they're working toward: that Carlo, having met those criteria, will resume his own money management. (Deal accepted; signed and dated by Dad and Carlo.)

Father will:	Carlo will:	Completed when:	Goal:
pay off card, charge 2%, defer payments, mentor Carlo	use debit card only, not borrow, accept mentoring, pass Banking and Credit tutorials	positive cash flow, no bank penalties for 1 year	Carlo takes over own bill paying

Carlo's side of the Deal is spelled out in the two middle columns. One lays out the preconditions for *getting or maintaining* the Deal and the other the criteria for *completing* it. The fourth column is the goal both sides are looking forward to as a specific outcome.

In this as well as the other examples we'll look at, you will notice three unwritten psychological goals, the most important purposes of any Deal:

- To stop money being an issue in your relationship with your young adult.

- To build basic skills, knowledge, and lifelong habits for prudent money management.

- *And*, as I said in the previous chapter, to transform your relationship into one of parity:

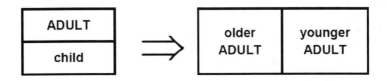

That third bullet point is the real gold. Your job is to build the learner's confidence (self-esteem), and thereby transform your role in his or her life from Annoying Parent looming over the child on the left side of the diagram—parent who must be used, manipulated, and circumvented—to Trusted Partner in Productive Growth. We'll discuss that transformation more fully in Chapter IV.

Now let's look at the explicit parts of your written Deal.

Specific goals

What are your biggest concerns about the way your youth handles his or her money? Answering that question will lead to specific goals. What needs to change? The insufficient earnings? Overspending? Failure to plan? Neglecting to pay bills, or complacency about the consequences of that neglect? Or the delusion that money grows on trees? Before reading on, get a sheet of paper and make a list of specific targets for change. They will guide your thinking about what conditions to require on the youth's side of your Deal.

The actual conversation with him or her, though, should begin on your side: what do you offer?

What support?

One option you have is to go on subsidizing them and keeping your fingers crossed. They're bound to grow up eventually, right? I wouldn't count on it. Help them get on their feet, yes—but you need to see behavior change.

At the other extreme, how about tough love? Cut them off without another penny? Let the school of hard knocks teach what happens to the reckless and inattentive? You may need tranquilizers, and an unlisted phone, but you won't need this book.

I'm assuming the third path: you're willing to support your youth with *mentoring*, as well as money—and *they'll only get the monetary support on condition that they accept the mentoring.*

Money is far from the most important thing our grown-up or almost-grown-up children still need from us. They continue to need the basics: the artful parental balance between giving them attention and giving them space. And as much as ever, they need us to build their confidence. Hopefully, from childhood on we've planted a secret agent inside them: their self-esteem.

Nonetheless, we can't avoid the fact that money is our best, sometimes our only leverage with young adults. Although they need our love, respect, and emotional support most of all, those aren't our leverage. Those gifts are unconditional. And *advice* about their activities, passions, friends, travel and so forth is often unwelcome. But they still need and welcome subsidies from time to time, and that's when they're most receptive to guidance about major purchases, leases, tax requirements, and skills they ought to have learned already, such as managing a checking account. If your kids *don't* need your help with money, why are you still reading? Take a long, expensive cruise. You've earned it.

Magic Triad

There are three things children need from parents as they make the transition to adulthood, even more than they need monetary support.

MOTIVATE: Parents can remind them of the payoffs for persisting to meet the challenges of a harsh world. Sometimes we even add incentives for responsibility, reliability, frugality, patience, and education, because the outside world doesn't necessarily reward such virtues consistently.

TEACH: Our job is to confront them with economic realities while instilling the skills and knowledge needed to improve their situation. Unrealistic self-confidence, without the requisite knowledge and skills, is a hindrance to development. We need to convey, through our sincere belief in their *realistic* abilities, that they're fully capable of the next step.

SUPPORT: Money is the least of it. We're here to help in many ways, short of undercutting their self-reliance. And more than money, they depend on our emotional support. Ultimately, that is what grows their confidence in their own abilities.

For those who do need our help, we'd be undermining their growth if we kept writing checks to them and for them without seeing more financial responsibility from them.

Instead of focusing on what bothers you about your young person, ask yourself what support he or she *needs*, that you're willing to *give*. This might include a monetary gift or loan, but what else? Perhaps just helping them monitor their bill payments and bank balance online a couple of times each month. Or teaching them basic concepts about debt (Chapter IX) and risk management (Chapter XI).

Here are some decisions to make about your side of the Deal:

- Do you want to make a *gift*, or a *loan*? (Chapter X) Think about which would be more useful to this young person in the present situation. A gift is more generous, of course; but it's not supportive if all it does is bail them out of a spot they

17

created for themselves. A loan might be more instructive, and less enabling of unrealistic spending. Another consideration is that a gift may imply a family precedent. Two years from now, will your younger child remind you, "You gave Michelle $2,500 to furnish her apartment; where's mine?"

- Whether it's a gift or it's to be paid back eventually, would it be better to hand over a lump sum now, or dole it out in the form of a weekly or monthly allowance?

- If the subsidy is for bills, should you help out by having those bills sent directly to you, so the youth doesn't have to deal with them at all? Or, depending where he or she is on the learning curve, will it be more useful to put the money in their account and let them handle the bills?

Then there are the non-monetary forms of financial support:

- free use of a parent's asset: condo, car, club membership; or rent-free living in the parents' home.

- free services: bill-paying, doing taxes, laundry, baby-sitting. (Surprise! She didn't need a credit score to get pregnant.)

- mentoring: supervising the learner's performance of certain functions (banking, taxes, job applications)—perhaps using www.EarnTrust.net, the suite of interactive tools we designed.

- employing the youth in a business you own or manage (see box).

Preconditions and completion requirements

As illustrated above in Carlo's case, the learner's side of the Deal will include two components: the preconditions (in order to get the support you're offering); and the completion conditions (in order to "graduate" from this Deal). In a simple case, you'll pay your daughter's rent for twelve months as long as she uses a joint account to deposit her paychecks and to pay, with your mentoring, her other bills. The agreement to accept your checking account

---

The dynamics of family business

Virtually all advisors in the field of family business suggest setting some eligibility criteria for family members to work in a company you own or run. Many owners require the next generation to work elsewhere and adjust their lifestyle to the reality of their earning capacity, before letting them apply for any full-time position in the family business. Most importantly, when they do meet the criteria for a position, start them with realistic expectations. A damaging mistake many owners make is setting family salaries according to the "needs" of the members' lifestyles, rather than the market value of each person's contributions to the business.

I've been consulted by many business owners about conflicts that arise when they bring sons or daughters into the business. Hiring them is a form of parental support, so it's more than reasonable to put some conditions on it: "This is the Deal." But frankly, I question why you'd hire a young person in your business if they're having the kinds of difficulties that we designed this program to help. Just as marriage is never a solution to a stormy relationship, employing an irresponsible son or daughter is never a solution to parent/child mutual frustration.

---

supervision is the precondition. "Twelve months in the black" is the completion condition. Earning your trust, and more privacy, is her reward.

The goal

The last component of the Deal, explicitly noted on the paper you sign, is what you both hope the outcome will be.

Let's look at some fuller examples.

EXAMPLE: A high school student. Hope is looking forward to her senior year of high school. Because they live in a suburban area where driving is a necessity, it's convenient for her parents to hand over the exclusive use of her Dad's car. (He's buying himself a new one.) But they want Hope to learn the realistic costs and responsibilities that come with an automobile, and they want to give her an incentive for taking good care of it. So her father says: "Hope, we'll pay for the insurance on 'your' car. You're responsible for all maintenance, gas, towing, parking tickets. Whatever value is left in the Subaru when we sell or trade it in will go toward your own purchase of your next car, or into your savings account." Hope puts her signature on the Deal. Notice that this isn't a case of intervening with a kid who has been irresponsible with money. Her father proactively proposed the Deal as an instructive experience, to teach Hope about the maintenance costs and depreciation of an automobile:

Dad will:	Hope will:	Completed when:	Goal:
provide car, pay for insurance	maintain car, pay operating costs	decision to sell car (perhaps when she goes to college)	Hope gets residual value of car

EXAMPLE: A college student. After their vague arrangements lead to frustration and arguing, Mom and Dad negotiate a written Deal with Paul. They agree to pay tuition each semester, as well as his one third share of rent in an off-campus apartment, airfares to and from college once each semester, and $300 per month toward other expenses, so long as Paul has passed all classes the previous semester and is enrolled for a full load of thirty hours. They also pay dental and medical expenses. Paul agrees to take care of everything else out of his part time earnings or, if necessary, his savings account. All this is typed out, signed and dated by Mom and Paul.

Parents provide:	Paul must:	Completed when:	Goal:
tuition, $300/month, one trip home per semester, medical care	enroll full time, pass all classes, pay all other expenses	college graduation	end parental monitoring

EXAMPLE: Moving toward financial independence. Marian is glad to accept a little monthly tutelage in bill payment and expense forecasting in exchange for her mother's postponing her loan repayment obligation. Mom also co-signed an apartment lease and bought Marian's car in her own name, though Marian writes the car loan and insurance checks. She pays all her current expenses, including insurance premiums and health care costs. She keeps documentation of her income and deductible expenses in orderly file folders, and makes her required quarterly estimated tax payments. Now she is taking out a charge card, which she'll use only for purchases she can afford to pay in full each month.

Mother will:	Marian will:	Completed when:	Goal:
postpone loan repayment, co-sign lease	accrue no other debts, keep mature financial records, make 1040-ES payments, pass Credit and Tax tutorials	mother is repaid	financial independence

EXAMPLE: Financial supervision. A college student, Josh pays his bills (rent, utilities, phone, Internet, car payments) and goes over his bank account each month under his father's tutelage. Together, they look at how much cash he went through and what his needs will be in the weeks ahead. Although the parents cover his food and books either directly or indirectly (by depositing the needed funds in his account), Josh has responsibility for entertainment and other discretionary categories out of part time earnings. His parents take turns as banking mentor. He and they do online banking and reconciling together. Because Josh abused the debit/ATM cash privilege in the past, they put a daily limit on the card until further notice. (Deal signed by Josh and both parents.)

Parents will:	Josh will:	Completed when:	Goal:
deposit in bank to cover specific bills	limit discretionary spending to his earnings, use debit card	demonstrates reliability with bank account and passes EarnTrust.net Banking tutorials	Josh managing checking account without supervision

EXAMPLE: Debbie doesn't get it. Deb blithely pronounces herself "engaged" to a nice young man who is employed in a low-paying job and can't afford to start paying off his college loans. Deb's parents know she has thousands of dollars of credit card debt, increasing every month. She knows they contributed $20,000 toward her brother's wedding last year. Can she plan on an equal amount? The parents wonder about the logic of throwing an expensive party for a young couple who may receive fine cookware and table service for twelve but won't be able to buy food. "Let's see your latest credit card bills," her Dad says. "All of them."

Parents offer:	If Deb:	Completed when:	Goal:
to coach Deb out of debt, no commitment to pay for wedding, but instead, will match her debt payments	destroys card, pays off debts before any wedding reservations	neither Deb nor fiancé has credit card debt, she passes tutorials on Loans and Banking	parents to consider contributing toward wedding expense

EXAMPLE: A wealthy trust beneficiary. I want to show you that this process, making the Deal explicit, is valuable for all kinds of situations and issues. Pete's late grandfather put a million dollars in trust for him, years ago. The trust specifies that the trustee can use funds for Pete's health, education, and maintenance beginning at age twenty-one. To keep this a parent/son example, let's say Pete's mother, divorced, is the named trustee.[2] Pete only knows vaguely about the existence of this trust, but after his twenty-first birthday—three weeks from now—Mom will be legally required to give him an annual accounting of the trust's current value and to consider prudently any request he makes for a distribution, based on what she considers to be his best interests.

Mom has mixed feelings upon learning from her family's money managers that the current value of Pete's trust is about $2,700,000. Unlike his younger brother and sister, Pete has a history of spending every dollar he ever got his hands on, beginning in childhood, when he insisted on the latest Nintendos and basketball shoes, all the way through the three years of college he squeaked through before he was suspended as a consequence of a police raid on a fraternity party. He hasn't gone back, and in the last eight months Pete held a job for only

---

2   A trustee needn't be a parent to use this approach. Chapter XIV deals with mentors who are not the youth's parent.

six weeks, traveled for eight weeks, and managed somehow to live in Vail for most of the ski season.

Pete's father, who doesn't have an inherited fortune of his own, does fortunately maintain good communications with Mom. They exchange emails and agree about their main concerns:

- They don't want to free Pete from the necessity to work at this stage of his life. (Although Mom's lawyer says she could legally define "maintenance" to include all food, shelter, clothing, and recreational expenses, she won't.)
- They want to encourage Pete to leave the bulk of his money in the trust, though they wouldn't object to letting him learn the hard way what will happen if he tries to invest a small portion of it on his own. They don't want him to buy or start a business before he's had experience working for others.
- Finally, they don't feel their two younger children are ready to handle knowing the size of their trusts. The only way to keep that secret is if they can persuade Pete to waive his own right to the information for a few years.

Accordingly, Mom and Pete make the following Deal:

- Mom will authorize tuition for any accredited educational program Pete enrolls in, full or part time.
- If he prefers to buy a house or condo rather than renting, the trust may be used for a down payment up to $100,000.
- Mom will approve withdrawals from the trust for unrestricted purposes, only up to an amount matching Pete's earned income.
- They add that the family accountant will prepare Pete's personal taxes and work with him year round to maintain pay stubs, work-related expense records, and so forth. Mom herself will mentor Pete on the bank account and personal bill paying he's responsible for. It's anticipated that a few months of mentoring will get Pete up to full authority over his checkbook. After living within his generous means for twelve months, he can choose either to pay all his own bills or

take advantage of the family office for that service. (Signed and dated by Trustee and Beneficiary.)

Trustee Mom will:	Pete will:	Completed when:	Goal:
match earned income, pay tuition if needed, buy home if desired, mentor Pete, explain Trust terms, authorize accountant for tax matters	live within means, pay own bills, maintain secrecy about Trust assets	12 months without money issues	Pete allowed option to use family office for bill paying eventually, more liberal distributions

Boundaries

Writing the Deal explicitly, perhaps in the form of a table like those above, is the best way to ensure that your young person can trust you to limit your meddling. You're pledging to stay within the boundaries of the Deal, leaving them in charge of everything else in their life. For example, if your Deal limits Marla's use of the ATM or debit card to a daily maximum of $50, that means she's free to spend up to $1,500 cash per month (if she has that much) without accounting for it. It's not your business how she spends it. Nor would you buy groceries for her if that day's cash went for a salon session.

If they come looking for advice, be sure to frame your advice in terms of "If I were you." Keep repeating that it's their decision and that you have neither a right nor desire to control their life beyond what they agreed to in the Deal.

Within the Deal's terms, however, be prepared to enforce consequences. (More on that in a moment.) And it's important to quit nagging, which never worked in their lives. All it did was maintain your relationship as a *nagging* relationship. Henceforth, it could drive an even bigger wedge between you. If your Deal specifies that Marla has to have her previous month's bills paid (as you'll confirm online) before you'll send your contribution toward the rent, and then she lets the due date pass, don't nag. Just let the chips fall.

Don't even think about nagging.

Stop it, now, stop it.

Nick's endorsement:
I have to say that Dad has been known to nag me and my sisters, even when he thought he wasn't. But the concrete clarity of our written Deals allowed us to remind him when he overstepped his bounds, what was our own responsibility and not his.

Reluctance to restrict

The problem we parents have isn't a matter of not knowing. We're smart enough to know we should reward children with freedom when they show responsibility, and restrict their freedom when they don't. The problem is that we *don't like* being restrictive. We want life to be *easy* for our children (and for ourselves). We also want them to see us as angels of opportunity and wizards of delight, rather than wicked witches and stern taskmasters who spoil their fun.

Younger children need limits in order to be safe, as well as a frame within which gradually to master new skills. When they were young and underfoot, of course, we had an additional reason to impose limits on what they did, where and when. We restricted them, not only to protect them but to preserve our own sanity. Now that they're out of our house—or trying to leave—they need us to be less protective. But that doesn't mean lifting all restrictions. We have to let them experience real world consequences for behavior, which sometimes means being *more* restrictive (less indulgent). For example, in the real world there is a cost to borrowing money. Interest is a *rate*: a cost over time. The longer you have the use of someone else's money, the more you have to compensate them. Maybe it's not a good idea to shield a young adult, or even a teenager, from that aspect of reality.[3] If you charge interest—say, 2 percent to 4 percent per year—on a loan to your child, might that be called "strict"? Yes. Is it being mean, to do so? Not if it helps your youth learn about the time value of money.

The principle is this: responsible performance leads to freedom. The preconditions and ongoing conditions probably do restrict their freedom in some way, in exchange for your support in money and time. What criteria do they have to meet in order to get free of that restriction?

Since money equates to freedom (in youth, at least), sometimes the reward for fulfilling their part of the Deal may be monetary: significantly more money, to the tune of a car, a house, or distributions from a trust fund. But in other cases, the freedom is simply the fact that you'll *ease off* from overseeing how she manages her checking account, and you'll trust her to make her own choices. Whether the learner sees the goal as a monetary one or simply as more independence, the important thing she'll have earned is your trust. Priceless!

When your child was young, you had the authority and the responsibility to make rules as a parent. But authority is no longer the basis of your Deal. If your youth were independent financially, you wouldn't be in the position to make a Deal. You could *hope* they respect your wishes, but when they're no longer under your roof, on what basis can you *insist* on anything? You're not going to withdraw your love, ban them from visiting, or refuse

---

3   We discuss this in Chapters IX and X.

to acknowledge their offspring as your grandchildren. So, like it or not, your only leverage does come down to material things.

Nick gets over it:

The hard facts of the world ground away my idealistic rebellion against Dad's definitions of responsibility. Eventually I realized that money models real resources, time, and human effort. It's a scoreboard for something truly important: the pride of *EARNING* my way through life, spending only what I can afford, applying discipline and effort to provide the resources for myself and, someday, my family.

My big delusion had been thinking that the concept of money was unjust, or simply not cool. Frankly, as I habitually "rebelled" against the system by allowing debts to accrue, I wouldn't have survived if my parents hadn't bailed me out a few times.

Who mentors?

You don't have to be a parent to guide a young adult using this system. Although I suspect most readers of this book are parents, I'll often refer to you as mentor or coach in the following chapters, because they're mainly about the teaching aspect of your relationship. (Chapter XIV discusses having someone other than yourself—a family accountant, for example, or a grandparent— serve as mentor for your youth.)

If you are one of the learner's parents, whether married or divorced, your Deal might differ from the other parent's Deal with that child. Communication and consistency between parents is desirable, but less crucial than with younger children. With younger children, family rules were *house* rules; the adults in charge of each home needed to enforce them jointly and consistently.[4] At this stage, though, the rules are about money and time that you

---

4   Kenneth Kaye, *Family Rules: Raising Responsible Children*. iUniverse, 2005.

may spend individually. The other parent might not have a clear, consistently followed Deal as you do. Therefore, specify whether the contract you're negotiating is a youth/parents Deal, or youth/father or youth/mother or learner/whomever. (Unfortunately, if the other parent or a grandparent is an *unconditional* funding source, you have less leverage.)

Negotiating the Deal

Conduct this process as you would negotiate a business contract: a proposal, then a counterproposal (both in writing, if more than a sentence or two), exchanging back and forth until you have a final version signed by both parties.

I find it best to open your discussion with what you are bringing to the table: your side of the Deal, anything from the privilege of living in your home to replacing a catastrophic credit card debt with a long-term parental loan on generous terms. Whatever you're offering, the approach is, "Here's what I'm (or we're) willing to do to help you. But only if you agree to …" whatever.[5]

Use real world consequences, in principle. Of course, your Deal is about helping, not about making a profit. So its terms will usually be more generous than those in the outside world, as in the example of a loan at 2 percent per year. Make consequences and conditions as close to the natural ones as feasible, and confine them to what really concerns you.

> EXAMPLE: Your daughter asks you to co-sign a lease and help her with the security deposit. She hasn't had any problems managing her bank account. So your Deal is simply about the apartment. It will probably involve, as a precondition, that she demonstrate an understanding of lease terms and of your respective responsibilities when you co-sign it. Although she'll have to pay attention to her bank account as she's handling the higher rent and utilities, you don't need to impose conditions

---

5   There's a detailed example of negotiating a Deal in Chapter V.

on her checkbook, debit card, or anything else that wasn't an issue in the past. Assume she has your trust in that area. If a problem develops, you can address it under the terms of a new Deal.

Following through: my double guarantee

To be enforceable, your Deal (like any contract) must be clear and specific (which means written!), and must deal with observable events. Parental restrictions at any age are only effective when constructed in such a way that fulfilling them leads the youth to more freedom. But *the parent must be prepared to follow through either way*: either with the promised result when completing conditions are met, or with *no* more freedom, perhaps more restrictive measures, if they aren't.

The greatest benefit of having made the Deal explicit comes if the learner, to your mutual disappointment, doesn't fulfill his or her part. Now the written Deal stops you from reacting punitively or critically. Let the Deal take the heat for you, instead of making it a power struggle: "Let's see what we agreed to: hmm, the Deal says you lose your debit card because you didn't leave enough in the account to pay monthly obligations. Sorry about that."

The most difficult part of any family counselor's job isn't figuring out what's at the root of a child's problems. It's convincing parents that the best thing they can do to help their child is to follow through with consequences when he or she tests the clear rules or contract they made. Having counseled at least a hundred parents who did and at least a hundred who did not follow through (not to mention having fallen in both categories myself), I can give you two guarantees:

- I guarantee that if your Deal was reasonable when you made it (for example, you set some conditions for contributing to your twenty-three-year-old's rent, and she failed to keep her part of the Deal), the most constructive, loving thing you can do is to pull the plug on that subsidy.

- My second guarantee, which I can't emphasize enough, is that *if you don't follow through, you will certainly prolong the problem and very likely make it worse.* It's called *enabling.*

Now you can see how important it is to think each situation through carefully when creating a Deal. Ask yourself (and the other parent if he or she is a partner in this Deal) whether you (both) can be trusted to follow through. Try to anticipate how the challenge will come. When my wife and I told our son we didn't care what passing grades he earned, but we'd only shell out for college as long as he got credit for every course we paid for, we had to be prepared to pull the plug the first time he got an F. (Which he did, and we did.) Ideally, your children already trust that you'll follow through with consequences, because you earned that trust by doing so with ruthless consistency when they were young. Even so, they may well test you again at this stage, and you'd better be prepared to pass the test.

Suppose the disappointing event happens. Your son doesn't keep his half of the college Deal, for academic or other reasons. Has the Deal failed? Not at all. It may not have met its stated goal, but it succeeds in its *purpose* when you follow through, letting that better teacher, experience, do its job. Now you need a new Deal. For example, "Before we pay for you to re-enroll at your college or anywhere else, you need to replenish the money wasted on that course you failed."[6] The student works for a semester, replenishes the college fund, matures a bit, and returns with a more realistic attitude about his and your investment in higher education. Or

---

6   If this sounds harsh, you're forgetting how difficult it is to fail a college course. A student has to go to extreme lengths, missing many classes and practically every assignment. In Nick's case, it wasn't about the difficulty of his New York University courses relative to his abilities. It was about getting out of bed in time for a 5:00 PM class. Other parents of other students would make a different Deal from ours. After pulling the plug, our new Deal was well designed to motivate our son: He would receive a modest rent and food allowance for the next year, so long as he worked to earn the additional costs of staying in the Big Apple. Which he did, eventually (after living hand to mouth for awhile, as he'll recount in later chapters).

31

maybe he doesn't go back, but takes a more productive direction, for him, at this point in his life.

Changing the Deal

Any of the examples above might prove to have been optimistic. The outcome both of you hoped for hasn't been achieved. That doesn't mean the Deal exercise failed, only that the parents and young people need to circle back and make a new Deal covering the situation that exists now. Sure, it's a step back from how close to grown up you and they hoped they were. But now, in light of the facts, they agree to more realistic, if slower, steps toward independence.

> EXAMPLE: Daniel hasn't held up his end of the Deal. You follow through with the consequence: you end the relatively generous, loose terms of that Deal. But you can make another Deal, imposing a bit more supervision, or reduced financial support, or curtailing your support for the less constructive part of his lifestyle (maybe he's not ready to live off campus, for example) while continuing or even increasing your support in other ways for the growth of his competencies and self-confidence.
>
> Let's say you're in the situation we faced, but your kid's circumstances and history are different from what Nick's were. You're willing to agree to a new Deal: Daniel can stay in school for now at your expense, but he'll owe you reimbursement for the course he failed. Alternatively, maybe you say he'll have to make up those credits needed to graduate, paying *that* tuition out of summer earnings.

The bottom line

The Deal is a contract about your support in time and money. It's never about your emotional support, which is unconditional.

Make your Deal with your young person explicit:

- What monetary resources and non-monetary (including mentoring) support do you promise to *provide?*

- On what *conditions?*

- *How long* will this continue, either in months or in terms of an observable result?

- And how will your learner's life *change*—whether through a monetary event or freedom in another form—if and when the Deal's terms are completed?

The rest of this book is devoted to making the experience positive for both parties to the Deal. It needs to be useful and easy during the time it's implemented, as well as good for the learner in the long term, and for your relationship. After an interlude by Nick on trust, I'll return to talk about what we're advocating from a psychological point of view. You have in your hands more than just a bunch of sound practices. You'll find it's a *systematic* approach to the transition from dependent childhood to mutually trustworthy relationships.

III. Life Lessons about Trust

by Nick Kaye

At seventeen, for about six months I took leave of middle class life and lived as a total vagrant, rolling around with this group of kids—we weren't exactly bums, but if I said we were self-supporting it would not be true. Some of us were crashing at this college guy's loft on Chicago's North Side and there were a couple of girls there who could cook, so this one kid—we called him Klepto Bob—would go to the grocery store and steal all the items on their list and bring them back, and they'd cook us dinner and let us stay there.

With Klepto Bob, you never knew when you would suddenly have to take off running. I didn't realize, at the time, that the thing to do in a situation like that is just let the other guy run. One day at a restaurant he suddenly whispered "RUN!" and I turned around and he had the gumball machine, taking off fleeing. I should have just stood there like I didn't know who he was with. You don't want to be running with a guy who's carrying a gumball machine.

In truth, he was a really nice guy. He just had this psychological problem where he didn't apply the Golden Rule. Basically, that part of his philosophy having to do with other people's rights was missing. He would just giggle about it.

I told my parents I had a job designing and painting this mural at an Irish biker bar. I may have neglected to mention, at the time, that I was paid in beer and burgers and whatever else happened to be consumed there. That was a great experience, hanging out at seventeen with biker guys ranging from about forty to seventy. The most incredible characters rolled through there. The guy who owned it, Jack, was in his forties and wearing a cast on his knee from snowboarding down Clark St. after a blizzard, on a tow rope behind a jeep. The jeep turned a corner, and his snowboard smashed into a curb. Jack had grown up in an Irish gang, duking it out with the neighboring Polish gang. So now he had a bar, and I was in there every day painting that mural for two or three months.

Jack's stories were informative, but the best characters were all the old road dogs that kept coming through, seventy-year-olds who lived nowhere, out of a pack on the back of their Harleys. Crazy, tattooed out dudes from the Sixties who were still trafficking drugs across the country. Met this guy who lived in a van, ·in which he had an office with a printer and an incredible archive of tattoo designs, his catalog. He would travel around to tattoo shops, find out what they had and what was selling, collecting art from artists all over the country.

Just hearing those guys' ridiculous stories, plus learning in general how to hang out with older people, altered my paradigm a lot. I didn't have any overhead at that time of my life; I'd finished high school early and didn't have a plan except that I was accepted at New York University. I suppose my interim plan was exactly that: a time to be a vagrant punk kid, freeloading food. An unscripted interlude, a bit of life.

This loft we were boarding at was an awesome space, with hardwood floors and an entrance direct from the street, and the roommates were all in college and knew a lot of people. So we decided to throw a party. The way it happened, I was working at that biker bar, painting the mural, and they were paying us in kegs. So, in order to survive we had to throw this party to convert beer into money. We had deejays, I performed some live music, and we actually made money at it.

Some time after that, hanging out, we met another kid, Dave. We must have mentioned to him that we had thrown a party and we're getting ready to throw the next party, everything's coming together. I didn't know this kid Dave for more than a week, start to finish. But by Friday night we throw another party, he's in our crew, right? He's helping us. It's wildly successful. At 8:00 Saturday morning the sound system is still bumping, everybody agrees we're going to go home, shower, nap, and come back. Invest the money we made last night, roll back to the bar and buy more kegs, everyone get the word out, get even more people in the door. And we threw it again. So then we had a double stack of cash. This is something I was fiercely proud of for about two seconds. Our boy Dave, the one we barely knew, was at the door holding the cash box. That blows my mind now, that I would be that stupid. I remember playing back mental videos to myself of how I could have prevented what happened, by just acting on what crossed my mind when I saw this look on his face. When I turned around he was gone, forever, with all our gate proceeds.

Of course, Dave was homeless: we met him on the El train. But we were essentially homeless too, though in his case it might not have been by choice. To this day, the ongoing story of my life has been an optimistic perspective based on the world I want to live in. The world I wish that we all lived in. Trusting people. There have been so many situations where I placed trust in people that I later regretted. But, you know what? On the whole, I don't regret being an optimist. There were a lot of situations, growing up—and this could still happen, the feeling is still there—when Dad suggested to me that someone I was spending time with was a less than constructive influence, or in some way was draining my time and energy. I would get very defensive about that: Who are you to judge my friends? I don't regret that I insisted on making my own choices of who to hang with and who to trust. The cultural diversification alone was worth it.

IV. Money's Not the Answer

> *Whether we decide to relieve our young adults' shortage of money or not to do so, they need three other things more: motivation, education, and emotional support.*

As much as we lose sleep over money, argue with spouses about money, knock ourselves out for money, we all know this: it doesn't buy happiness, you can't take it with you, and it's the root of at least some (nowhere near all) evil. The title of this chapter means something less obvious, which we need to talk about before going on with the details of our system for helping a young adult overcome money trouble: *Even when the problem seems to be money, money isn't enough.*

"How much do you need?" a father played by Jason Robards in the movie *Parenthood* asks his hapless son (Tom Hulce), with a look that says "... you worthless, disappointing, lying bum"— while reaching into his pocket.

As a psychologist as well as a father, I wanted a way to communicate exactly the opposite. A way to give my sons and daughters the consistent message, "You're worthy, you're capable of succeeding, I love you, and we're going to help you." A system that helps by teaching them to fish rather than merely handing them a wad of fish.

EMT: Earning Mutual Trust (not just Emergency Money Treatment)

Money may well be part of your Deal, as we said in Chapter II. But money is only one component of the support you'll give. And support is only one of three elements this system requires from parents and other mentors, whose job is to build the youth's

- motivation, which includes trust that the outcome will be worth the effort;

- education, the skills and knowledge that make his or her self-confidence realistic;

- support, "my family is here for me" emotionally as well as financially;

- belief in Self, confidence that "I can do this."

That last need, confidence in one's abilities, derives from all three of the others. So we can think of the mentor's input as a magic triad: Motivate, Teach, and Support. No one of those, without the others, leads to mutual trust. All the incentives in the world won't help without the teaching and emotional support. A thorough knowledge of money management concepts and techniques won't change behavior, without motivation and positive messages from parents and coaches. Nor will expressions of support and confidence, alone, be enough.

Put simply, for our young adults to earn our trust by becoming independently responsible, we have to earn their trust by being reliable motivators, teachers, and supporters.

Motivate

When we say a person is motivated, we're saying more than that she has a desire for something. We're saying that her *actions* reveal a strong drive. She doesn't merely *want* to be elected to office, or win a sports trophy or get a particular job. "Motivated" means she's putting her energy and self-discipline into attaining that goal. Conversely, if she says she's motivated, but makes no visible effort toward the goal, she is lying to herself.

What makes some young people pursue their goals, often in the face of repeated failures and obstacles, while others retreat to the couch with the TV remote as soon as the going is tough? To say that one has more motivation than another is only to beg the question: why?

Parents and teachers do more than build children's knowledge and skills directly, through sequential steps, They do as much, or more, indirectly by building self-confidence ("I believe I can handle this") and self-esteem ("I'm worthy of a good life"). The diagram from my book *Family Rules*[7] shows how the child's increasing abilities feed confidence and self-esteem, and all three fuel continued learning.

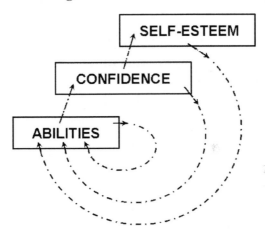

For some young people, what holds back motivation is uncertainty about how much to expect out of life. Harvard psychiatrist Robert Coles used the word *entitlement* for a quality he found in the attitudes of children in affluent families. This was something rich kids shared across different regions of America, different religious and ethnic groups, conservative or liberal. Unlike children living in poverty or trauma, the affluent children's experience led them to believe themselves *entitled* to the better things in life. They assumed that they'd be comfortably well off as adults. Coles pointed out that entitlement has both an upside and a downside, as has certainly been my experience in working with many wealthy families.[8]

---

7   Kenneth Kaye, *Family Rules: Raising Responsible Children.* iUniverse, 2005.

8   Consistent with these observations, recent researchers find that affluent American teens' sense of entitlement leads to better school perfor-

Children with a healthy dose of entitlement can pursue goals with confidence. They easily envision themselves in positions of influence and security, similar to what their parents enjoyed. Since they expect that all needed resources will be available for their education, travel, sports training, business capital, or political campaigns, they can be confident that their own effort to study, practice, or compete will yield results. They're also motivated to learn about managing wealth, so they'll be prepared when wealth comes to them.

> EXAMPLE: Alex (one of a number of motivated young men and women in the wealthiest families I've worked with) went through college in four years, captained the lacrosse team but also worked every summer: once for money, and twice as a six-week volunteer with the forest service in Montana. Each of those two summers, he spent the other month traveling with friends. Alex majored in psychology, but plans to apply to business school after working for a few years. His first job after college is an internship with an environmental organization. "I'm fortunate that I don't have college loans to worry about paying back right away," he tells me. "Most of my friends do."

Sometimes, though, affluence can have the opposite effect. Not that it's the *cause* of depression, low self-esteem, or anxiety; those symptoms can arise in any developing child or youth, for whatever combination of biological and situational reasons. Wealth affords no protection from them. When they happen to hit a young person in an affluent family, he or she may begin to feel undeserving of the easy life. "Why me? I don't deserve all this. I didn't earn it, and I wouldn't be able to earn it on my

---

mance, but emotionally they are more anxious or depressed, less able to cope with stress, and less self-reliant than working-class youth: Dan Kindlon, *Too Much of a Good Thing: Raising Children of Character in an Indulgent Age*, Hyperion, 2001; Annette Lareau, *Unequal Childhoods: Class, Race, and Family Life*, University of California Press, 2003; Madeline Levine, *The Price of Privilege: How Parental Pressure and Material Advantage are Creating a Generation of Disconnected and Unhappy Kids*, HarperCollins, 2006.

own if I had to." So they feel worse about themselves than a less fortunate child does. They feel *un*entitled.

Often, lack of entitlement is a more or less unconscious feeling, not openly admitted. What do such children and adults do? They rely on the things money buys—the toys, the collections, the clothes and superficial friendships—as reassurance of their worth as a person. They may act as if they felt an *excess* of entitlement, but it's a pretense.

> EXAMPLE: Ricky was the last of four children in an entrepreneurial family. His father had built from nothing, by the time Ricky was in college, a $30 million manufacturing company with an international reputation. The oldest son, like their father a workaholic with only a high school education, had been instrumental in growing the business, along with a sister who'd earned an MBA. Another sister was a physician. "Ricky was the best student of us all" was how they expressed their disappointment in him. An accounting major, Ricky had three challenging job offers upon graduating. Instead of pursuing one of them, he saw the family business as a quick route to income and perks. He actually told me, "I was looking at entry level jobs where I'd be making half the money and working twice the hours."
>
> Over the course of years as I tried to help this family with serious conflicts between the generations, I watched Ricky grow obese, more depressed, lonely, and reliant on material purchases as tokens of self-worth. His absences and lack of effort made him his family's scapegoat in battles about the future of their business.

> EXAMPLE: One of my suite mates in college was a prince, literally (kid brother of the crown prince of a small European country). He took some of us out to expensive restaurants, showed us magazine spreads of his family's castles and sports cars, brought in a decorator to furnish his dorm room. He was a sad figure who left in the middle of our second year despite good grades in his pre-med courses. Trying to use spending as a pick-me-up, the depressive grows more depressed, the

anxiety sufferer more anxious, and the low self-esteem youth even lower in self-esteem. In The Prince's case (we used his title ironically), free-spending and generosity didn't buy him any real friends, only ridicule behind his back. It turned out he wasn't spending real money, either: as The Prince waited with his luggage for a taxi to the airport, a truck arrived to repossess the furniture he had charged.

The solution? First, we need to recognize that a youth who expresses doubts about his or her entitlement and one who acts the opposite (*over*entitled) are both lacking in motivation and probably both suffering from self doubt, which *money cannot cure*. What they need is assurance that they're valued for *anything but* money and the things money can buy. Imagine someone saying to you, "I really enjoyed spending this time with you, because you're rich." Would that make you feel good? But if they said, "… because you're thoughtful" or, "… because you make me think," or "you have a unique perspective," "you're *kind*" or *a good listener* or *funny* or *original* or *generous* or *helpful*? Whatever sincere, specific compliment someone can give us—specific enough so that we know it's sincere—is priceless, isn't it?

All this suggests that the external incentive—the monetary reward being sought, or the car or house or whatever it may be—is the least important element in motivating a young person. What we really hope for in our children is *internal motivation*: that they be self-driven and self-disciplined. And this requires meeting those other two needs at least as much as we motivate them with material incentives.

How do you make someone feel their effort will pay off? That the goal is worth attaining, and they're entitled to go after it, and they'll succeed at the tasks involved in reaching that goal? Clearly, a big part of motivating is strengthening a child's belief in herself. To counter negative messages the world may have given her (or she may be giving herself), it doesn't help merely to say "You're capable, you can do it, you'll make it." One must identify

---

Preventive advice for parents

Janet Bodnar, *Raising Money Smart Kids* (Kiplinger's/ Dearborn, 2005)

Eileen and Jon Gallo, *Silver Spoon Kids: How Successful Parents Raise Responsible Children* (McGraw-Hill, 2001)

Joline Godfrey, *Raising Financially Fit Kids* (Ten Speed Press, 2003). This highly readable book suggests skills children should attain by each stage from preschool through high school.

Neale Godfrey and Tad Richards, *Money Still Doesn't Grow on Trees: A Parent's Guide to Raising Financially Responsible Teenagers and Young Adults* (2004). Despite the last words of the title, this book deals mainly with giving teens the information and advice that will keep them from getting into financial trouble.

Kenneth Kaye, *Family Rules: Raising Responsible Children* (iUniverse, 2005). Available in its third edition through the major online booksellers, *Family Rules* deals with ages two to eighteen, not primarily about money issues;.

Jayne Pearl, *Kids and Money* (Bloomberg, 1999). Also about young children through teenagers.

---

something she has genuinely accomplished, as evidence for what you know she can do in the future.

> EXAMPLE: I had a chance to sit in on an executive coach's session with a thirty-two-year-old sales manager for one of my clients. The coach, let's call her Barbara, specialized in helping business people with time management and organizational problems. Although his sales manager hadn't been clinically tested, my client, a sixty-year-old entrepreneur, recognized the manager's distractibility and impulsiveness as probable symptoms of adult attention deficit disorder (ADD), because he had it himself.
>
> A few minutes into the meeting, Barbara remarked that the young woman had said "I can't" five or six times. "I know," she said. "I shouldn't be so negative. But it's true, I'm helpless at organization. I just get paralyzed."

"What's the best thing you've done for the company since you've been in this job?" Barbara asked. The manager thought for a few moments, then replied that she had reduced the amount of detail in the call reports her subordinates had to write up daily and submit to her every week. After asking her to explain what this involved in the company bureaucracy, Barbara commented, "That sounds like an organizational task."

"Yes, but it was a high priority for me because I hate doing call reports myself."

"So we've disproved the idea that you *can't* get things organized; it's really a question of what makes you charge ahead in certain situations and give up in others." She continued the interview in that vein, using the woman's acknowledged successes to buttress her belief in herself.

Is that only a technique to use with employees who have ADD? Of course not. It's basic counseling for anyone whose low confidence blocks their learning. In fact, it's basic parenting.

Motivation is almost impossible without belief in self. The most exciting incentives in the world—the promise of a Ferrari, say, if the student gets straight A's for a year—won't motivate them to work harder unless they believe they're capable of that achievement.

EXAMPLE: I learned a lesson from an adolescent patient who couldn't list the months of the year. His parents, both college educated—Mom was a high school teacher, in fact—had brought Steven to family therapy because of behavior problems in his ninth grade class. In addition to acting out, he wasn't doing homework assignments. The parents obviously needed help setting and enforcing rules. They, and I, wondered what they could do to motivate him.

When I met privately with Steven, he was evasive and morose. He seemed to be of average intelligence—until, by chance, I discovered he didn't know the months in order. I happened to mention something happening in April, and he asked me when April would come. "Today's March 23," I answered. The fourteen-year-old simply looked blank, and when I failed to disguise my astonishment, I embarrassed him (not my finest moment as a therapist). Then it turned out he couldn't list the days of the week in order, either.

I began to realize, and later helped his parents realize, that Steven wasn't skipping school and throwing away homework assignments out of defiance to authority; he was doing it out of shame. It turned out he had a specific learning disability, which hadn't been diagnosed. It had led him to believe he was stupid (wrong), and that his parents were extremely disappointed in him (true). The first of those beliefs was easier to change, once thorough testing clarified the nature of his disorder. The second belief was more difficult. I had to teach the parents to recognize and praise the few things Steven did well, and while holding him accountable with consequences for his misbehavior, start distinguishing between the behavior and the person.

Nick: Believing I could do the job

My first job in the adult world was a summer job when I was sixteen, in the main offices of Ameritech. I got hired to work on their website, only because my brother was the head of that department. My boss, who was about forty years old, reported to my twenty-eight-year-old brother, which didn't help me feel less nervous.

The first day, the guy handed me a four hundred page operations manual with a million tabs all down the side, in a binder, and told me to make an exact replica of the thing. I was hired because I knew HTML coding; I had no idea how to do this adult task that was presented to me. But I came back to him two days later without having asked anyone for help or advice, with an exact replica. I just broke that task down like an assembly line, and executed it. Which, basically, is what I've found to be successful any time an assignment overwhelms me: break it down into layers.

At the end of the summer, that boss told me he threw both copies away. It was an expired manual. From the perspective of a guy who'd been managing

cubicle farms for twenty years, and was asked to
hire his boss's little brother, he wanted to test
how sharp I was, and more importantly, whether I'd
whine about it.

Teach

Imagine that you boost your kids' self-esteem all their lives by
praising everything they do. Suppose they believe you, that they
can achieve great things, yet no one provides the actual knowledge
and skills they need. For example, in the money area, they don't
understand how interest payments work and they believe the hype
that says credit cards are a way of saving money through discounts
and postponed obligations. It doesn't matter how optimistic their
beliefs are: without the basic training, they'll fail.

A huge amount of misinformation about economics floats
around among young adults' peers. I have been astonished at
how strongly a young person may insist he or she really does
understand the credit system, or taxes, or investment, while
staunchly maintaining basic misconceptions. Correcting their
understanding meets with resistance because it's a challenge, not
only to their own sophistication, but to that of the friend who
misinformed them in the first place.

For example, I find most young adults firmly believing that the
best or only way to establish a credit rating is by going in debt to
a credit card company and paying the minimum monthly balance.
(We'll devote parts of Chapters IX and XI to that problem.)

What about your kids? Do they know ...

- how to calculate the marginal value of a purchase to the
  purchaser (for example, when a more expensive car might be
  more economical)?

- how to calculate the actual cost of a purchase when
  borrowing is required (the cost of the loan as well as the
  price)?

Books about money

For teens:

Arthur and Rose Bochner, *The New Totally Awesome Business Book for Kids* (Newmarket Press, 2007)

Nancy Holyoke, *A Smart Girl's Guide to Money* (American Girl, 2001)

Robert Kiyosaki and Sharon Lechter, *Rich Dad Poor Dad for Teens* (Little Brown, 2004)

For young adults:

Brian T. Jones, *Getting Started: The Financial Guide for a Younger Generation* (Larstan Publishing, 2006; for young adults)

Jeff Opdyke, *The Wall Street Journal Personal Finance Workbook* (Dow Jones/Three Rivers Press, 2006).

Suze Orman, *The Money Book for the Young, Fabulous & Broke* (Penguin Riverhead Books, 2005).

- the concept of opportunity costs (what am I giving up by spending this money in this way)?

- how checking accounts work (minimum balance, time to clear, what happens in the case of insufficient funds, how does one prevent that)?

- how interest works: in a savings account and as a borrower?

- pros and cons of secured loans versus unsecured loans?

- how insurance works (auto, home, health)?

Other types of knowledge for which parents can be the principal mentors include:

- risk management: from backing up computer disks, to door locks and fire protection, to preventive maintenance on a car;

- home economics, especially how to shop for food and prepare meals (Nick says none of his friends learned this at home);

- if they have a trust or other invested funds, what this means and will mean over the years;
- how to present themselves on job applications;
- pay stub deductions and reporting;
- leasing an apartment.

We'll talk about all of those in later chapters. Let's consider one concept now, as an example: the concept of opportunity costs. Someone who has been eating nothing but restaurant and take-out, or delivered pizzas, can easily save $600 a month by preparing at least two of their meals each day themselves. That seems elementary to an adult. Believe it or not, the relationship between a few dollars and a large monthly savings is the kind of mental development that many young people understand only in principle. They don't really see it applying to them.

A one pack a day cigarette habit costs about $225 a month: $2,700 a year.[9] How much will that cost you over ten years? It depends what you'd have done with the money instead of smoking it. If you stuffed $225 under your mattress every month, assuming you didn't have a fire or a robbery you'd find $27,000 under that lumpy mattress after ten years (with diminished purchasing power, due to inflation). But suppose you put $225 per month into an investment fund with a 6 percent annual return after taxes: in ten years, it's worth $37,282. In other words, a pack a day smoker over ten years burns through enough money for a down payment on a house; not to mention the effect on her health.

We'll talk about other budgetary considerations in later chapters. My point here is that if kids aren't educated about the realistic costs of their purchases, the time value of money, and the arithmetic of interest rates, they are headed for money problems even if they do try to be responsible.

---

9   State taxes vary greatly, so I used the average retail price in California for these calculations. Two thirds of all cigarettes are purchased in convenience stores, by the pack rather than in cartons.

Of course, teaching doesn't just consist of providing good information. It consists primarily of putting learners in situations at the growing edge of their confidence, allowing them to learn by inquiry and by trying new things under supervision. Then one reinforces their successes with praise, and points them on to more training.

Support

I've said money isn't enough. Throwing money at the money-challenged while ignoring those other three needs will most often exacerbate their problems. However, poverty is a black hole, almost impossible to escape without financial help. So you are going to provide that help, only *not by itself*. Help implies caring. Make sure the right message comes across with your financial support.

> MISTAKE: In the scene from *Parenthood* that I mentioned earlier in this chapter, the father asks his son "How much do you need?" in a tone that conveys how fed up he is. The clear implication is, "You've done it again; this is typical of you; I expect nothing better from you." That isn't supportive, no matter how deeply the parent reaches into his pocket.

> BETTER: "I'm prepared to help you learn how to work your way out of debt and stay on top of your expenses. It isn't easy. We'll have to take a thorough look, together, at what you're doing to make a living and where your money's going. Do you want my help with that?" In other words, Deal? Or no Deal? Whether the youth chooses to accept the Deal or no, the parent has shown support by offering.

Enabling isn't support!

We need to be frank: recreational drugs are a feature of many young people's lives, understandably troubling to parents. Drugs and alcohol are major items of expense, but even when they're free (supplied by friends or roommates, for example), they can be the enemies of productivity and monetary discipline. So we won't ignore the role a bad habit may have played, and may still be playing, in getting your child into financial troubles.

Not ignoring it, however, doesn't mean it's always best to confront it directly, as you would with a teenager or younger child. Now that they're quasi-independent, in many cases your most effective parental strategy will be indirect: concentrate on your youth's difficulty in making ends meet, and let them connect the dots between that difficulty and their recreational choices. In fact, the financial effects of a chemical dependence may be fortunate from our point of view, because parents are on firmer ground to exert leverage when kids are broke. I'll describe the indirect approach first, followed by the direct assault on an addiction, and let you decide which one fits your situation.

The "wait and see" approach: indirectly using your Deal to break denial

Suppose you suspect that a bad habit—alcohol or drug dependence, most often, but it could be any compulsive behavior—plays a role in your learner's money problems. Maybe it's the expense of the habit itself, or the interference with their employment, or the fact that insobriety leads to irresponsibility about bills and checks and so forth. But they aren't in trouble with the law, they're in school or working full time, and none of their friends or siblings have hinted that there's an issue. Your suspicions may very likely be correct, but trying to address them wouldn't be effective. It might only drive a wedge between you and the kid you're concerned about.

Am I saying you need to wait until they hit bottom? Try to ignore the problem, as the young person seems to want you to do? Not exactly. I'm saying that until *they* are feeling a crisis, you can only influence that problem indirectly. The *financial effects* of a budding substance abuse habit are what you can address directly. Don't pretend not to know it's going on—but skip the sermons. Take the position that only they themselves can decide when it's a problem requiring change. On the other hand, you're not in the business of subsidizing that choice in their life. Which means that when drugs deplete their resources, you're not going to subsidize the resulting shortfall in other areas .

How do you find out whether a drug or alcohol problem (or a gambling addiction) is at the root of a young person's "money disorder"? My advice is, you don't have to go investigating. Until such a problem rises to the level of a crisis in itself, you can do more good by directly addressing the money issues.

EXAMPLE: Carly and her friends call themselves "party animals." Her parents know she smokes marijuana, and not only at parties. At twenty-one, living with three of her friends from high school, she makes no secret of going out and "getting wasted," with a frequency that concerns her parents. Has it gone beyond recreation? Who knows? They smoked their share of pot at her age, and still sometimes drink more than they intended. But when Carly tells them she can't make ends meet, and shows them her monthly income and expense numbers, they suspect the party budget—including alcohol and other substances—is more significant than she's reporting.

MISTAKE: Her father tells Carly, "With the paychecks you're depositing every two weeks, you should be able to cover rent, food, car, clothes, CDs, and everything else. The fact that you're getting further and further behind tells us you're not being honest—with yourself, perhaps, but certainly with us—about how much you're spending on booze and drugs, as well as money that's slipping through your fingers when you're wasted." He takes too strong a position for these circumstances, threatening to cut off her subsidy until she changes her lifestyle. Why is that a mistake? It's actually what I'll recommend in more severe cases, but in this case he has nothing that would prove the point *to her*. She is likely to deny the problem and to resist her parents' views, if not dismiss them as hypocritical.

BETTER: It's fine to raise the question with Carly about the impact of her partying, but once asked, drop it. You lose credibility yourself if you claim to know more than you do. Instead, I would try to provide what she's open to: advice and mentoring as she tries to make ends meet. Using the "Banking 101 and 201" mentoring we describe in Chapters VII and VIII, help her see the reality of her cash flow position. For example, she's earning $1,500 a month after taxes and has $1,200 in fixed expenses, leaving only $300 ($10 a day) for food, transportation, and non-essentials. Let her come to conclusions herself about the partying. Whether the problem really is an addiction, or merely the wrong friends, or insufficient motivation to resist them, her lifestyle has to prove itself untenable—to her.

If Carly were to point out that her parents are party animals, too, a constructive answer could be, "We don't spend our rent money on partying." But keep the focus on helping her sort out why her income isn't enough to cover her expenses.

Fortunately, drug and alcohol dependency in the young often creates or contributes to financial irresponsibility long before it escalates to a medical crisis. So the first sign of a possible problem may be bounced checks or neglected utility bills. Those are red flags—at least orange alerts—but you still needn't get into the lifestyle question. Your opportunity to make a Deal based on the youth's living within his or her means is more likely to lead to positive effects on decisions about recreational drug use than any lectures or threats you could make on that subject.

EXAMPLE: Mike doesn't drive under the influence, he shows up for work every day, rarely drinks to excess, and he only smokes marijuana in the evenings, with friends among whom it's as casual a social lubricant as beer. He claims it's not a problem. He's just broke.

MISTAKE: His parents argue that it is a problem. It's illegal! Mike insists that law enforcement only concerns itself with drug *dealing*. His parents have entered an argument they can't win. They won't be able to shake his denial about the danger of addiction.

BETTER: Accept that Mike believes it hasn't yet become a problem. He may well decide for himself, at some point, that his time on the couch is a waste of what should be productive hours, or that partying is the reason it's too hard to get up for his early morning job. Either he'll curtail his recreational using before it becomes a serious problem, or there's a good chance his increasing dependence will lead to a money crisis. While his friends can afford the drugs they're buying, Mike cannot. Sooner or later he has to buy his own, especially as his consumption goes beyond what's shared at parties. Now it's a significant expense. He doesn't acknowledge the fact to his parents, but drug buying makes him short on his living expenses. It's that crisis, in turn, that gives the parents leverage to spell out a Deal with Mike: they'll bail him out with a loan, as long as he accepts their temporary help with his bookkeeping and bill paying, and limits his cash access to what's left over after the basics are paid by check. (The process will become clear in subsequent chapters.)

Parents will:	Mike will:	Completed when:	Goal:
Loan enough to get phone and internet reconnected and this month's bills covered	Pay monthly bills first out of each pay-check, then a minimum of $100 back to parents	Loan repaid and all bills are paid up	Mike doing banking and bills without Mom's help Mike living within his means

Some months later, the Deal "fails". That is, it succeeds in forcing a crisis, breaking Mike's denial, giving his parents more leverage to insist on a professional evaluation, which may lead to a chemical dependence treatment program.

In another kid, it might not be the out-of-pocket cost of his "recreational" drug, but the fact that he starts getting in to work late and loses his job, or he starts using during the day and takes longer to finish freelance assignments, or he has the money but lets his bills pile up or loses them, his electricity gets shut off and he can't get on the Internet, misses email from clients, and so forth. In other words, cash flow deteriorates. Now the question is, as you're working with him on the money problem, should you insist on knowing—honestly—how much he spends on drugs? My answer may surprise you: *no, you shouldn't, because that won't work.* He's already lying to himself anyway about those costs. Unless the problem rises to a crisis, you don't know for sure that he's in the grip of a drug problem. Pushing a son or daughter whose drug dependence is at a deniable level will only undermine your chance to be helpful.

Don't pretend to be naïve. Acknowledge that while he thinks it hasn't become a problem, you believe it already has. You might say, "I think you're going to find recreational drugs are incompatible with your budget." But leave it at that. Don't make any ultimatums you can't enforce, and don't ask a question that they can't, or won't, answer truthfully.

Rest assured, you're not enabling the problem, as long as you don't subsidize it or pretend to believe his denial. You're merely giving him the opportunity either to limit the impact of his recreational choices, or to let them get out of hand to the point where you'll intervene more directly.

In other words, make financial responsibility the primary agenda, your front line, so to speak. I assure you that deciding to stop nagging about their lifestyle doesn't mean you yourself are in denial about a possible addiction. It's simply that as long as they're far from hitting bottom, you direct your energy to the mentoring that will either

- eventually make the costs of their habits (financial as well as personal costs) more salient to them, thus breaking through the denial; or

- have such good effects on their self-esteem and motivation that they get off the couch and, without further intervention,

---

Beyond Deals and money matters

I want to be clear that the leverage you have, to negotiate a Deal about money with your child, is not a treatment for substance abuse, other addictions, or for any other mental or emotional illness. All of those call for professional diagnosis and specific treatment programs.

Although the advice in this chapter may help in confronting a young person with the financial consequences of his or her lifestyle, I would not use such confrontation with people whose primary problem is depression, or a reality disorder (hearing voices, for example) – even if their money management deficits resemble examples in this book. In those cases, as with the case of the indubitably drug dependent, put this book aside and seek psychiatric advice.

---

keep their recreational behavior within bounds and outside your concern.

My experience is that with someone of adult years, drugs should be addressed when the problem is severe enough so they can hardly choose to ignore it: when denial is already breaking down. Then you stop all pretense that the kid might be able to keep the "recreational" drug use under control. You also stop pretending that what they need most from you is money management training.

Intervention

As long as young adults' addictions are only a possibility or even a probability, focusing on their chronic shortage of money can be a way to motivate lifestyle change or lend force to their own dissatisfaction. But if addiction becomes indisputable, and people are in that phase of denial where they acknowledge the problem but want to believe they can moderate the behavior, pointing out its financial costs isn't likely to break their denial. More powerful confrontation might take the form of setting up a facilitated intervention, together with other family members and friends. It might begin with your "tough love" refusal to continue subsidizing them at all. (While you offer to help, to the extent you're able and willing, with the cost of detox and rehab.)

> EXAMPLE: Britney, twenty, is a single mother, living in the apartment over her parents' garage with her two-year-old daughter. Her mother watches the child while Britney works the 4:00 to midnight shift in a factory, five days a week. Often, Britney comes home at 5:00 or 6:00 in the morning, too tired to do anything with her child except put toddler videos on and doze on the couch. When she's awake, there's always a beer in her hand. She had one DUI in her teens, before her pregnancy; didn't drink for nine months but laughed that "I can't wait for this kid to pop out so I can drink again." Several times, Britney's too hung over to function at all in the morning, or passes out in the afternoon. She has missed more than her allotment of sick days, so her paychecks are now short due to absences and late punching-in, and the employer has put her on notice that she may lose her job.
>
> MISTAKE: Britney's mother offers to pay off the credit card debt and assume all her diaper and food expenses, to relieve Britney's financial pressures. Mom envisions a Deal along the lines of Chapter VII, where she'll mentor Britney on check paying and help her analyze her expenses. It's too late for that!
>
> BETTER: Address the problem head on. Britney certainly has reasons to be depressed, exhausted, and disillusioned about her life, but she needs to be confronted with the fact that her "solution" is making all her problems worse. This is, admittedly, a very difficult case. With the baby, the parents are unlikely to evict her. But whatever Deal they make with Britney has to require her to go through rehab and stay sober. Otherwise, loans and financial mentoring would only prolong and worsen her problems.

Similarly, if the young person is arrested, or loses her license after a second drunk driving conviction, or the problem escalates to the point where friends and family are talking about how to intervene, it's definitely time to stop focusing on teaching her to manage her bank account better, or to work her way out of debt.

This applies to other addictive behavior as well, such as sports gambling, or Internet poker, even playing the stock markets with money one can't afford to lose. Counselors ask questions like the following to assess whether someone is addicted to gambling: "Have you ever spent more money gambling than you intended to?" "Have you ever lied to any one to hide the amount of gambling you are doing?" "Have you ever had to borrow money to continue gambling?"

Whatever the type of addiction, when you decide it's incontrovertible, address it directly. Put this book aside and forget about coaching the poor kid to manage money better. Put the addiction on the front burner and, with a concerted effort by everyone who cares, do all you can to get the addict into treatment. The first or second intervention may not work, if the child is legally an adult. Use tough love—withdraw all support—no more Deals. (As I mentioned, it's probably a mistake to reward the addict with money for going into treatment. Addicts are manipulative, and if they don't really want help, the treatment will fail.)

The bottom line: patience and sensitivity

All kinds of circumstances lead young people to be money-challenged. Many have attention deficit or learning disabilities. Others are more than capable of learning the skills and routines of managing their money, except their parents took those skills for granted, perhaps assuming kids would learn them in school (rarely true, unfortunately). Still other children, suffering from low self-esteem, seek gratification or peer approval by spending beyond their means.

Then there's the grandiosity of the young: illusions of invulnerability. They left the nest prematurely, perhaps for love, or to make babies, or to seek fortunes. Their only failing was not being pragmatic. The predatory credit industry encourages their delusions, because they're the best kind of borrowers: "nonprime," meaning forced to contract high interest rates.

Lastly, either in combination with the foregoing or as a main cause, drugs or other addictions contribute to many young people's money problems. Let's face it, drugs—not just beer—play some role in most young Americans' lives. Yours may have stopped hiding the fact from you, now that they're technically adults. On the other hand, perhaps there's no sign that they use drugs at all. Maybe they don't. That's why I say, focus on the money unless a drug problem has led to the kinds of trouble where addiction is undeniable.

The system I'm offering in this book covers a range of young people's money problems, whatever their cause. Make an inventory of the magic triad I discussed in this chapter: Motivate, Teach, Support. Which does your child especially need?

If the problem is a lack of motivation, you can remind them of what they're saving for, or studying for; or you can create additional incentives in your Deal.

If the problem is doubt about their own abilities, remind them of things they've already accomplished. But also make sure they do have the needed skills and understanding (Chapters IX and XI): train them yourself or find another mentor for them.

Finally, think hard about the kind of support you've been providing. Is it the kind that undermines self-reliance, or enables them to deny their own bad habits? The right message of support is this: "I'm here for you if you fall down—and want to change."

V. The Place Where, When You Have to Go There, ...

> *"Home is the place where,"* Robert Frost wrote, *"when you have to go there, they have to take you in."* Having an adult child still at home with you, or returning for awhile, can be a plus for both generations. Just make the Deal clear.

A friend joked that I should title this book *How to Prevent Them From Moving Back Home*. That surprised me. It wouldn't have occurred to me that there's anything necessarily bad about twenty-somethings living with their parents. It happens frequently, and is only a problem if the Deal isn't clear to all concerned.

After all, extended families have shared a household as the normal mode of human life, from prehistoric times to the present. In some cultures it was expected that young men bring their wives to live permanently under the same roof or in the same compound with their parents and brothers. Other cultures went the opposite way: young men moved to the extended families of their wives. Either tradition served the purposes of economic efficiency and passing the culture from generation to generation.

As social organizations became more complex, rules relaxed about who lived where. But for centuries—until the mid-twentieth century in the U.S.—it remained common for a family of three or even four generations to live together on a farm or in a house or apartment, or migrate together in search of work and opportunity. In most of the world, this is still the case today: households including infants up to great-grandparents. As the middle aged couple grows less able and the next generation more able, leadership of the household passes to the latter. As the young children become numerous and the older ones are able to help with chores or productive labor, only then do their parents and uncles and aunts break into separate households.

Are there tensions? Sure. These relationships require constant clarification of roles, mutual adjustments, tolerance and patience. But that's life. What's unprecedented and difficult is our highly mobile society, with its expectation that, after a prolonged adolescence devoted to education and a kind of pretend independence, young adults should suddenly be able to support themselves in homes of their own.

For many, it's unrealistic to think they could get a job right out of school and immediately obtain and furnish their own place, cover rent, clothing, and food, buy and maintain a car or truck, get health insurance and start paying student loans. All that, while just beginning to figure out who they are and how to hook up with their soul mate for life. True, some of us did all that at twenty; but not without mistakes and pain.

It's no wonder we parents of young adults look at the empty bedrooms in our own homes, or the basement space that could be converted into a semi-private apartment, or the investment property that's currently tenantless, and see a way to help our kids save some money when they're getting started in the world. In the 2000 census, fourteen million American families had a grown child living at home. The number is surely rising as this book goes to press, with a downward economic spiral unprecedented in our lifetimes.

And let's be honest, part of us wants them back. We live for those times we can be together as a family. We like to see our children (when we're not arguing with them). They're bright, energetic, idealistic, and funny—or they're depressed or in bad health and we're concerned about them. Either way, we want to be with them. If we're fortunate enough to be able to help our youth and see them more often, why not?

Just be sure to remember what we said in Chapter II, and work out the Deal that is genuinely in your youth's interest as well as your own. Make sure it's Win/Win.

It won't help him if it leads the two of you to argue when he expects you to do his laundry and never chips in for groceries. It

---

It's all across America

In a small town diner in South Dakota, I overheard three farmers chatting. "My daughter called from California," said one. "They were about to be evicted. I had to send a thousand."

"Only a thousand?" another farmer said. "That's just the first installment, let me tell you."

"It mighta been a mistake," the first man said. "Now they'll just stay out there and get more ass deep in debt."

"Yeah, I been there," the second man said. "We're paying our daughter's rent. Son-in-law's got a rig; hauls cars out of Billings. He made sixty grand last year, so he goes and buys a second rig for seven cars instead of four. Now he can't make two trips a day no more, because the turnaround takes too long, loading and unloading."

"If I let 'em get evicted," the first speaker said, still ruminating on whether his bail-out was a mistake, "maybe they'd come home."

"Would that be good?" asked the waitress, getting a laugh from the others.

"I told my wife," said the third man, "when the last one leaves town we best pack up, ship out, don't leave no forwarding address."

"You got that right," the first man began, then shook his head. "Except—she's got kids, you hate to see the little ones evicted and all that."

"How many?" the waitress wanted to know.

"Six. The oldest is only seven."

---

will help if your Deal includes some reasonable sharing of costs and other responsibilities.

Living with you won't help her if the money she saves on rent feeds a drug or alcohol addiction that will only get worse. (Even if her only drug is tobacco, do you really want to enable her $200 a month carcinogenic habit?) It *will* help if your house rules add structure to her life along with the shelter.

It won't help her if having a place to live merely prolongs her adolescence. It *will* if you treat her as an adult sharing your home.

(I'd encourage her to change rooms, if possible, rather than re-inhabit her childhood bed and furnishings.)

It won't help if you or he characterize his moving back home as a failure on his part. If you've decided it's for the best, then you should characterize it as a wise move. After all, if it's true that one in four young adults have had to move back in with their parents for financial reasons,[10] it must be due more to the reality of our economy than to failings on the part of all those individuals.

> MISTAKE: Joanie's parents give lip service to the wisdom of the move, but one of them makes a flippant remark about it to their friends. "We thought we'd have the house to ourselves now, but she managed to get herself evicted and turned up on our doorstep." Overhearing something like that can undermine any number of supportive statements.

Finally, it won't help if it's a good deal for the kid but bad for you. Your own resources may be limited. And even if you're financially set for life, you need to protect your turf, your privacy and relationships with your peers. There's no reason to let your home become a night club for under-thirties, a warehouse, or a youth hostel.

You're entitled to keep your house just as orderly or disorderly as it would be if your son or daughter weren't there. If you've come to a point in your life where your home finally looks like the pictures in *Sunset* or *Architectural Digest*, then that's how you should expect your young housemate to help keep it. On the other hand, if you're casual about dust or clutter, you wouldn't tolerate a guest or a tenant calling you a slob and nagging you to straighten up; so don't accept it from your youth, rent paying or not.

What services, if any, are you prepared to provide this young adult, besides access to some space? Here is a sample list to get you started:

---

10   Neale Godfrey and Tad Richards, *Money Still Doesn't Grow on Trees : A Parent's Guide to Raising Financially Responsible Teenagers and Young Adults* (2004).

Rent or mortgage payment?	
Heat, air conditioning, utilities?	
Telephone, internet, cable TV, security service?	
Home or renter's insurance?	
Food?	
Lawn care?	
Maid service?	
Laundry service?	
Use of vehicle(s)?	
Fuel for vehicle(s)?	

Your categories might be different, but surely you expect a contribution of *some* kind; if not in money, then in work. Not to do so would be treating your would-be adult like a little child or an invalid.

Let's see how one of my clients used the table in negotiating her Deal with her son. Diana was a working single mother who happened to be comfortably fixed, but wanted to stop enabling her twenty-two-year-old's illusions about what she called "the free ride." Ted had been sharing a San Francisco apartment with friends for two years after dropping out of college. He worked full time in a copy shop, but habitually spent more than he earned. Each month put him further behind in his share of the rent and deeper in trouble on his credit card. Eventually, his friends asked him to move out. Ted came back to Illinois, where he had no trouble landing a job at the local Kinko's. With no savings and almost $10,000 in debt to MasterCard and to the California friends, his best option was to move in with his mother.

Under the circumstances, Diana sincerely welcomed her son. But she wanted to be proactive and avoid arguments. Here's how she filled out the table above, discussing it line by line with Ted.

65

Ted would have his own bedroom and bath, and also use living areas of the house, so Diana figured a fair rent would be about 20 percent of what the house cost her. That would make Ted's nominal rent $600. However, so long as he came up with $600 each month, she would only keep half of that as rent. She proposed to apply $300 of it to his credit card debt each month. (Whatever he owed his friends was between him and them, not Mom's problem.) He was to pay her $600, and she'd then write a $300 check to MasterCard.

MONTHLY	$$ or time cost to Diana	used by Ted	$$ payment from Ted	non-$$ contri- bution
Mortgage payment	$3000	20%	$600 minus $300 rebated	--

Diana wanted Ted to recognize the other costs of living: heat, utilities, insurance and so forth. However, his presence wasn't going to increase those other expenses. So she agreed not to charge him for those homeowner costs, but she expected him to help control the bills by conserving energy.

MONTHLY	$$ or time cost to Diana	used by Ted	$$ payment from Ted	non-$$ contri- bution
Heat, air conditioning, utilities	$425	20%	--	Close windows, etc.)

Since Ted had his own phone, there was no reason he should answer her land line. The process of spelling out their Deal prompted Diana to make it explicit: "land line and voicemail for Mom's exclusive use." You might not have such an item on your list, but for Diana, it underlined the fact that this was her house.

MONTHLY	$$ or time cost to Diana	used by Ted	$$ from Ted	non-$$ contri-bution
Telephone, internet, cable TV, security service	$240	<50%	--	Phone, voicemail Mom only
Home insurance	$40	10%	--	--

When she brought up food, Ted said he'd buy his own and keep it on designated shelves. That didn't preclude either of them inviting the other to share something they'd cooked, but Ted didn't have to kick in for the grocery budget. Again: your Deal might be different.

MONTHLY	$$ or time cost to Diana	used by Ted	$$ payment from Ted	non-$$ contri-bution
Food	$800	little	Buy own food	--

This negotiation took place in April, when the lawn service was about to make their first weekly visit. How much or how little Ted would actually *use* the yard wasn't the point. Diana was giving up her long-awaited privacy and taking hardly any money out of Ted's paycheck. So she felt it was reasonable to ask him to save her the cost of lawn service all summer by cutting the grass every week. Ted agreed without an argument.

MONTHLY	$$ or time cost to Diana	used by Ted	$$ from Ted	non-$$ contribution
Lawn care	Was $220, now cancel	?	--	Mow & trim to lawn service standard

Now that two people would be living in the house, Diana's twice-a-month cleaning crew was even more important to her. She didn't expect Ted to chip in for that, but the Deal stated that he wasn't to litter the house with his stuff. "You're not a teenager any more," she said, though in terms of maturity she really felt he was.

MONTHLY	$$ or time cost to Diana	used by Ted	$$ from Ted	non-$$ contribution
Maid service	$320	20%	--	Clean kitchen after every use; keep own things in own space
Laundry service	--	0%	--	Do own laundry

Ted owned a car, so they recorded in the Deal that each vehicle was its owner's full responsibility. That could have gone without saying. Nonetheless, it didn't hurt to write it down.

MONTHLY	$$ or time cost to Diana	used by Ted	$$ from Ted	non-$$ contribution
Use of vehicle(s)	$200	0%	--	Won't use car
Fuel for vehicle(s)	$400	0%	--	Won't use Mom's car
Other: Mutt	$100	50%	--	Walk, feed Mutt as requested

I won't tell you that Diana never had a problem with Ted during his year and a half in her house. It was mixed: some fun, some aggravation. But the written Deal kept the arguments and nagging to a minimum. By the time Ted moved to Chicago and a new roommate situation (where he paid $850 a month), they'd reduced the credit card debt by half. Diana had paid off

MasterCard, to eliminate the exorbitant interest, and Ted was paying her back. (We'll discuss that in Chapter X.)

> EXAMPLE: Let's briefly consider a different scenario. At twenty-six, Melinda was surviving on her income as a part-time waitress while chasing her acting ambitions through unsuccessful auditions. She'd had a few short-term situations as a roommate with others, none longer than a few months. Now she was moving back home.
>
> MISTAKE: Putting no financial conditions on Melinda allowed her to imagine that she could support herself indefinitely with the waitress job, until her big break would come as an actress.
>
> BETTER: Since they preferred not to charge their daughter rent, her parents could say, "We expect you to accumulate what you save by not paying rent. You have to earn $500 after taxes, over and above what your food, clothing, and going out costs you. Work enough shifts to increase your savings account by at least that much every month, as a condition of living here."

Incidentally, under current U.S. tax rules, if your youth makes less than $2,750 for the year and you provide more than half his support (including the value of rent you're not charging him), you can probably treat him as a dependent on your income tax form – check with your tax advisor about that.[11]

The bottom line

You're doing the right thing if your son or daughter lives with you as a responsible adult, contributing whatever is reasonable to the household, whether that means contributing to the rent or merely sharing the work and consideration that cohabitation requires. Even if their mate or child is part of the package, sharing your home with them can be constructive and enjoyable.

---

11   She can't claim herself as an exemption on her own tax return and also be claimed as a dependent by some one else. Nor may two parents who file separately both list the child as a dependent.

It's a different story if your hospitality enables them to avoid growing up. If it pulls you back to the relationship you had as their caretaker-provider-housekeeper-nagger, you need to stop doing that, for both your sakes. What's the Deal?

VI. Attention Money Disorder

Attention problems range from clinically diagnosed, neurological differences in brain wiring that affect reading, memory, and organization in general, to habitual obtuseness and inattentiveness about money in particular. It's helpful to understand any of those as frustrating circumstances for the individuals as well as for their parents and teachers, calling for different approaches to the organization of the young adult's financial life. Motivate, Teach, and Support are still the names of the game—tailored to the strengths and weaknesses of this unique person.

A group of young people who often run into the kinds of difficulties we're talking about are those with attention and impulsiveness problems. Such problems may be connected with specific learning disabilities (LD) that lead them to avoid thinking about financial subjects, such as analyzing their income versus expenses, or managing a bank account. It's not that they aren't capable of the simple math those tasks involve. The problem may be that they lack confidence in those abilities. Or it may be that the way numbers are displayed on a bill or bank statement distracts them with too much digital information competing for their attention. Or the problem might be one of impulse control.

In fact, I think many young people who have *no* attention problems in other areas of their lives suffer from a non-clinical, social syndrome that might be called Attention Money Disorder: the tendency to pay attention to stuff they want to own or do, rather than what they can afford at present and is consistent with mundane planning.

We're not concerned in this book with diagnosing whether your young person has ADD (Attention Deficit Disorder) or ADHD (Attention Deficit Hyperactive Disorder), or neither. Boxes later in this chapter list some books and Web resources that could help them ascertain whether they fit one of those syndromes and if so, what to do about it medically, educationally, or through coaching. But with respect to the goal of helping them get on top of things financially, it hardly matters what clinical label does or doesn't apply to your learner.

Two things are useful to know about the whole group of attention and learning disabilities (or deficits or disorders or dysfunctions):

1. They aren't merely childhood problems. Difficulties persist through adulthood in at least half of those who had these extra challenges as kids. It's especially difficult if they weren't diagnosed in school, when the child could have benefited from alternative teaching methods.

2. At all ages, the individual with any of these syndromes is "uniquely wired," as many experts say. Treatment is not a matter of rewiring them. Medication can alleviate some of the difficulties, but by and large what they need are strategies and tools for playing to their strengths instead of their weaknesses.

Severity varies enormously. One individual might have only a mild form of dyslexia that makes it difficult to remember how to spell words but doesn't interfere with reading or other kinds of work, while another lacks the ability to process certain kinds of information (maybe math, maybe abstract concepts, maybe social cues), making him appear slow in one area while totally normal, or even gifted, in other areas.

Although I'm a psychologist, my motivation for reading up on ADD research[12] was a desire to understand my son and stop making things harder for him because of my own frustration. Nick

---

12   Contrary to what some anti-medication extremists have written, it's well established now in the medical profession that ADD is essentially a matter of neurological wiring, affects millions of adults, not only children, and is most often treatable by a combination of coaching and medication. However, we're not concerned with whether your young adult has had the diagnosis, or is getting specific help for the disorder. The advice in this book applies to any young person who needs help getting and staying out of money trouble.

got an A in every course that piqued his interest and allowed him to use his creativity. In classes that didn't interest him, he'd get C's, D's, or F's on some assignments, especially if a teacher insisted on a disciplined, uncreative adherence to rules: topic paragraph due Monday, note cards and outline the following Monday, five page double spaced first draft with one-and-a-quarter-inch margins ten days later, and so on. (David Giwerc, a prominent trainer of ADD coaches, calls the disorder "a challenge of boredom.") I had usually done well on assignments like that, and I've never had trouble managing my bank account, showing up on time for work, meeting deadlines. But that fact made it harder, not easier for me to be a helpful coach to my son.

There are numerous great resources online and in bookstores for people with ADD as well as for their parents (see box). There are also certified coaches, and you might consider whether one of them could be an effective mentor for your son or daughter in managing their money matters.[13] Alternatively, you might ask someone like your accountant to be the financial mentor instead of yourself, for a variety of reasons. Chapter XIV discusses delegating the mentoring role to someone else. However, you can't turn over your parental *relationship* to anyone. You still need to replace the message "you're a screw-up and I, your superior, am once again disappointed in you" with "I see your talents and I'm impressed with the effort you're making. All those positive steps you've made toward organizing your life will pay off in success."

AMD – Attention Money Disorder

This book involves only one aspect of the organizing effort. The kind of attention problems we're concerned with are problems in paying attention to earning, spending, borrowing and paying. I'm calling these problems "AMD" without making any assumption

---

13 Or for yourself: studies have found that if a child has ADHD, there's at least a 50 percent likelihood that one parent does, too.

about whether the original cause was neurological (for example, brain cells deprived of oxygen during birth), emotional (for example, depression), psychodynamic ("passive aggressively" challenging parental values), or inherited through the parents' genes. For whatever reason, AMD people possess any number of the following tendencies. How many of these describe your young adult?

- Frequently misreads financial information
- Assumes an understanding without seeking sufficient information
- Avoids reading material that involves financial calculations
- Has difficulty learning or applying math skills
- Poor grasp of abstract concepts
- Trouble filling out applications or other forms
- Has difficulty getting or staying organized
- Slow when work is very repetitive, or the opposite: slow at work that's always changing
- Inattentive to details, or the opposite: excessively focuses on details
- Poor at double-checking work
- Has difficulty making written notes from oral lectures
- Consistently forgets a particular type of information (names, dates, or appointments, for example)
- Makes surprising errors about relative positions (which of two numbers is greater, which of two dates is earlier, how long between two dates)
- Has difficulty seeking feedback (perhaps defensive due to years of criticism)
- Has problems negotiating for himself or herself
- Has difficulty resisting peer pressure
- Has difficulty empathizing with another's perspective

ADD and other learning disabilities in young adults - books

Anne Ford with John-Richard Thompson. *On Their Own: Creating an Independent Future for Your Adult Child with Learning Disabilities and ADHD.* Newmarket Press, 2007.

Edward Hallowell and John Ratey. *Delivered from Distraction.* Ballantine, 2005.

Thom Hartmann. *Attention Deficit Disorder: A Different Perception.* Underwood Books, 1997.

Mary Beth Kravetz and Imy Wax. *Guide to Colleges for the Learning Disabled* (4th Ed.) Princeton Review.

Jonathan Mooney and David Cole. *Learning Outside The Lines: Two Ivy League Students With Learning Disabilities and ADHD Give You the Tools.* Simon and Schuster, 2000.

Patricia Quinn, Nancy Ratey, and T.L. Maitland (2001). *Coaching College Students With AD/HD: Issues & Answers.* Bethesda, MD: Advantage Books.

John Ratey. *A User's Guide to the Brain.* Pantheon Books, 2001.

Nancy Ratey. *The Disorganized Mind: Coaching Your ADHD Brain to Take Control of Your Time, Tasks, and Talents.* St. Martin's Press, 2008.

° Misreads social cues (a raised eyebrow, for example)

If you checked a third or more of those difficulties, I want you to start thinking of your child (if you don't already) as an individual with special needs. He's *not* willfully rejecting all the wise counsel you've given for ten or twenty years. She's *not* disrespecting your values. They're *not* put on earth to undermine your financial security. They simply have surprising difficulties in processing information.

In a famous passage in *Huckleberry Finn,* Jim tells Huck about an event that he recalls with shame. His four-year-old had been ill with scarlet fever. After she recovered, Jim told her to shut a door, but the child just stood there, looking at him stupidly. The father repeated his order a few times and then, when she continued to defy him, slapped her. As she stood in tears, not understanding why her father had suddenly become enraged, a gust of wind slammed the door shut loudly behind the child. She didn't flinch. "The Lord God Almighty forgive poor ole Jim," he says, "cause he never gonna forgive himself as long as he lives! Oh, she was plumb deaf, Huck, plumb deaf – and I'd been a-treatin' her so!"

Many of us can remember charging our children with willful defiance when it turned out they were only oblivious. The children's behavior that pushed my own hot button was lack of consideration for others. When I thought Nick was habitually selfish and inconsiderate of other family members' needs and rights, I'm sorry to say I blew up at him more than a few times. A wonderful thing happened in our relationship when it gradually dawned that his unreliability wasn't selfish inconsideration at all. He's one of the kindest, most loving people I know, as long as his mind isn't focused elsewhere. Now that he has learned to rely on calendars, daily to-do lists and organized folders, he keeps appointments, remembers birthdays, returns calls as well as most people. More importantly, though, when he slips up—as we all do—his father reacts more often with compassion instead of indignation.

That's what we need to do with our kids' AMD—their money disorder—regardless whether they do or don't have a certifiable attention deficit or learning difficulty. They don't see things that may be obvious to you (unless you have the same problems). Perhaps you yourself only acquired money skills after great effort. You wish you could save your child all that effort. You can't. They need help. They need our patience, and they need us to do exactly the opposite of what comes naturally when we're frustrated with somebody: praise them.

Nick: The challenge of self-organization

Freelancing sounds fantastic—choose your hours, work from home, be your own boss—but the truth is, you'll have a dozen bosses competing for all your hours, making conflicting demands and chaining you to your desk. Furthermore, even when you have a great month and bill a lot of work, that doesn't mean you get the checks any time soon.

In the face of all that, the most crucial thing I've learned in business is to remain polite. No matter how angry or upset I might feel, success is directly related to calmness. The tough guy approach may have worked at some point early in human evolution, but it doesn't work in business. The first work I did for this one client, they gave me a check on the day I finished the animation for their website, and asked me back for another job. I thought, wow, this is a great client; but it was because they knew they needed me for the second job, so they wanted me to feel good about them. The next job, though, they took forever to pay. No one accepted responsibility for not having paid me. They passed the buck to someone in Payables who I wound up knowing better than I knew the people I had worked with. Finally, around the third or fourth time I called her, I was a little rude. I thought I'd caught her in a lie, and I probably had, but it was before I realized that everybody knows what everybody's bluff is and you don't call them on it because it's better to focus on your next move and do that. It's bound to be counterproductive to tell someone that she's inconveniencing me by doing her job. I said something like, "Quit jerking me around." At which point she got offended, and then made a point of taking even longer to mail my check.

Freelancing doesn't necessarily teach you what you need to know to deal with big businesses, with suits and office buildings and all. Those guys know what they're doing. Self-employment isn't big business and it isn't small business. It's little business, more like personal finance. It brought the problems I had with money right home to me in a big way. When you're a freelancer or a sole proprietor, you are more like a hunter-gatherer than a business. It's like being a small fishing boat, compared to a big ship with a working crew. You have to do all the jobs; you better keep your gear well organized and close at hand, and you better not need any sleep. On a large vessel, there's a whole organization in place providing for everyone, and rules and traditions and schedules.

Dos

Can you relate to the parents in this 2006 "news story" from the satirical *Onion* paper?

Visiting Parents Do Their Best
To Praise Son's New Apartment

BROOKLYN, NY—Parents of 23-year-old Jack Gambel attempted to put a positive spin on their son's new Brooklyn apartment Monday, referring to the one-bedroom railroad-style residence's location above a Chinese restaurant as "charming," and calling the exposed hot-water pipes "very New York." "And you won't have to spend a lot of time cleaning a bathroom this size," added father Dave Gambel, who agreed with wife Barbara that the 10 by 12 foot bedroom's lack of natural sunlight will help their son get a full night's sleep. ... Mrs. Gambel also noted that the thrift-store table in the "cozy" kitchen/television area/dining room was the perfect size for his father to write out a $1,750 rent check.

Many of us have been there, and (barring sarcasm) we were right to accentuate the positive. The most important thing we can do for young people who are struggling to support themselves is to be sure our financial support comes with an equal amount of emotional support.

Do emphasize your confidence in the learner's ability.

Do recognize and acknowledge good intentions.

Do acknowledge and praise every positive step. A young man who had a credit card told me, "I have paid every balance in full, for the last three months." That shouldn't be a big deal, but it was for him. "Fabulous," I said. "Most people don't learn to do that until it's too late and they're already in trouble."

Do spend extra time and patience giving them a realistic sense of actual costs (apartment, car, clothing and the difference between one's pay and one's take-home check).

Do say "No"

We often need to say "no": a friendly no, not a rejecting no. Why do our young people, even after they're well out of their teens, keep putting us in this uncomfortable position?

In many cases, this youth is entrepreneurial. He expects to do great things as soon as he can be his own boss, start his company, make a fortune. Working for others in the dreaded "corporate bureaucracy" doesn't work for him. All he asks of those who love him and desperately want him to succeed is that you invest money in his venture. Or at least pay his living expenses while he creates a fabulous business. He'll take care of you and the whole family, once he's made his billions.

Guess what? Many successful businesses began that way. Bill Gates was no rags to riches story: he had rich parents. He could afford to drop out of Harvard and start Microsoft.

However, the great majority of business start-ups fail. The entrepreneurs who start them and fail with them are just as smart and just as hard-working as your son or daughter. (Many will succeed with their second, or third, or fourth great idea, probably not with the first one.) A prudent parent might be wise to say, "I'm rooting for you from the sidelines, but I can't afford to risk any more of my own security." Or "The best test of how promising your idea and your business plan are is whether you can get backing from lenders or investors who don't already love you."

Unfortunately, it's not easy to remain positive about a kid with a track record of chasing dreams and behaving impractically. A natural reaction is to remind him of all his mistakes and failures.

Then he gets defensive, and starts insulting you (many ADD individuals have a short fuse): you're stingy, or obsessive, or harping; you never support him, you're always busting his dreams and putting him down. Accusations like that are so unfair they make you mad, and then *you* respond defensively.

> MISTAKE: "You haven't finished a single thing you ever started. You spend other people's money as if it grew on trees. You're like a bottomless hole we've thrown money down. Are you ever going to grow up?"

I'm all about bringing reality home to youth—but without insulting them. Negativity provokes defensiveness and denial, rather than the realistic self-assessment and behavior change we want. A more constructive confrontation with reality occurs when they look in their wallets and bank accounts and don't find the wherewithal to pay their bills. What they need most at those times is the parent who is *not* angry at them or contemptuous of them, and brings some tools to address the problem.

The experts on learning disabilities and ADHD can help us with those tools. As Anne Ford and John-Richard Thompson say, it is vital for parents to reverse the destructive message that youth with LD or ADD have internalized:

> For years they endured the frustrations, humiliations, and repeated failures in school .... Along with teachers insisting they didn't try hard enough and classmates calling them stupid, a great deal of damage is caused by self-criticism and the drumbeat of 'I'm not good enough' that plays over and over in their minds. They grow up, they go to college or enter the work force, and the drumbeat doesn't stop. It beats on and on to affect jobs, relationships, family life—everything.[14]

---

14   Anne Ford and John-Richard Thompson, *On Their Own: Creating an Independent Future for Your Child with Learning Disabilities and ADHD*. Newmarket Press, 2007, p. 184.

Great things are accomplished when children who happen to have these "challenges of boredom" receive encouragement from parents and teachers, praise for their creativity, initiative, energy or for individual talents that have nothing to do with attention and organization.

Richard Branson, the founder of Virgin Records, Virgin Airlines, and other extraordinarily successful businesses, recalls his childhood that way. Looking back at his adolescence, he identifies with the characteristics of ADHD but recalls no humiliations, self-criticism or nonstop drumbeat.[15] He seems to have been fortunate in his choice of parents. Others, unfortunately, find their own frustrations magnified by their parents' inability to believe that things in school can really be so difficult for them; the kid's not dumb, so he must be lazy.

Nor are criticism and frustration the only ways parents make difficulties worse. The parent who tries to compensate for a child's difficulties, smoothing the path, shouldering tasks for him, asking others to make special accommodation wherever he goes, can be equally destructive.

> EXAMPLE: A client of mine, a self-made single woman with only a high school education who had built a company with 200 employees, had alternately coddled her son and complained about him for thirty-five years. At fifty, he had the title of Vice President. As her only heir, employees assumed he was in line to succeed his mother as owner/CEO, a job for which he seemed qualified in intelligence, judgment, and better interpersonal skills than she had. But he only worked three days a week, nine to five. It was all he could handle, he said. Working with her gave him headaches. For years, she had paid him a generous, full-time salary, tolerated his putting in twenty-four hours a week to her fifty or sixty hours—and never let him forget it. (He said he would start working full time only when she retired and turned the business over to him.) My advice to

---

15   Branson's is one of several interviews included in Ford and Thompson's book, cited above.

her? "Tell him the truth. If you don't think he can handle your job, don't threaten to sell the business, just do it." She had been an amazing provider, of money rather than self-esteem.

I headed this section "Do Say No" because when children are having difficulties, their parents' reaction is often to give in, try to make life easier by saying yes, instead of acknowledging the difficulty and helping the child get around it himself. When you do say "No, you can't have this" or "No, you can't do that," don't let the message imply "No, because you're defective" or "No, because I'm disappointed in you." Say no because your kid is asking something of you that you can't, or don't choose to, do for him. And where the request is for money, don't pretend you can't afford it. Say simply, "That's not a use to which I plan to put my money. "

Like Richard Branson, and countless other entrepreneurs who struggled with learning or attention problems, our children's self-esteem will gain more from having met challenges and achieved goals through their own effort than from being given a free pass.

Here's some advice from the billionaire entrepreneur Charles Schwab, who learned at the age of forty-eight, when his ten-year-old son was diagnosed, that he himself had been dyslexic all his life:

Certainly in my case, as a child, I spent all kinds of time thinking about ways I could make money. I used to be one of those kids picking up Coke bottles at football games and turning them in for a nickel. I never saw a football game, but at the end of the game I'd end up with six or seven dollars in my pocket. In the post-Depression years, that was a great way to be measured. You'd get your self-esteem at that time through things like that. ... Nurturing and letting the child feel good about themselves, in whatever work they may be doing. In my experience, you have to start very small and work your way up ... a matter of collective experiences over many years.[16]

Do teach the use of checklists

ADD coaches offer numerous tools and organizational strategies, of which we'll mention one in particular: To-Do lists. They're useful for anyone, of course, but many people with ADD find them life-changing. I can't add anything to what Nick has to say on this subject.

Nick: My to-do list

I'm a poster child for the sub-type of ADD that I'd call Blissful Ignorance Disorder. I'm attentive to the details I choose to attend to, a good listener, always excited to turn my mind to new people and ideas, seldom bored in social situations. I'm a craftsman with a patient compulsion for perfection. But financial inconsistency has been a major problem in my life.

I've gone through work droughts when I should have watched my bills, overdue collections, and bank balance like a hawk. I continued to spend, just to keep my spirits up, treating dates to concert tickets, going along with friends to restaurants I couldn't afford, buying new gear. "No news is good news." I glimpsed the bad news on the horizon and told myself abstractly to spend "as little as possible." As the days went by with no money coming in, there were incidental necessities like tools and materials to loft my bed above a work bunker ($400) or a weekend trip ($500), and somehow, defying rationality, I'd sweep those items under the carpet until, lo and behold, when I finally login to my bank for the news report, it's another emergency!

The medicine I prescribe for my Blissful Ignorance Disorder may not make sense to you, but that's my

---

16   Quoted by Anne Ford in the book cited above, pp. 269-270.

point: each of us needs to find the system that works best for us. I've heard of people who rank their priorities under a whole bunch of categories, and I have a friend who retypes his whole list every day, removing the crossed-out items. Whatever works for you. What I do is force myself, once a month, to write out my entire life on a sheet of paper with checkboxes. It's divided in sections— Clients, Chores, Bank, Purchases, Travel, Fix— and a couple of those sections have subsections. Basically, it will be between twenty and thirty items with checkboxes next to them. They may look overwhelming—a cluster of minutiae—but this works for me because it forces the looming storm cloud of to-dos out of my head and onto one page. Tacked to the wall over my computer monitor, it's like a pilot's instrument panel. Each individual has to experiment to find what works for them. Right now, two of my unchecked boxes have been there for a year. Seeing them every day is a stinging reminder of how far I have yet to travel to full maturity. But what's the alternative? *Not* seeing them? It forces me to make decisions every day, at least to dispose of the urgent action items.

What really makes this method work for me is the checkbox, whose effect is magic: that moment of merciful Zen when I take up my black Sharpie marker and slay the empty box with a definitive **X** . Believe it or not, I check boxes in my dreams.

My whimsical artist's brain would rather sketch visions of alternate universes than get together a tedious bid for a new client, mail checks to subcontractors (much less landlords), or remember to take a deposit to the bank. But rain or shine, those checkboxes stare me down every day, dangling carrots. (I actually award myself prizes for checking off longstanding boxes: for example, permission to take a twenty-four hour vacation from my computer and clients when a long-nagging task is finally checked off.)

ADD in young adults – web resources

www.adultaddandmoney.com – weekly blog, with guest articles pertinent to young adults with money problems.

www.adda.org – the leading organization of adults with ADD and the professionals who serve them.

www.addca.com – training and certification for ADD coaches.

Don'ts

Don't nag! Just make "if…then" rules, and follow through with the promised consequences.

Don't let them provoke you into attacks.

Don't argue about the brilliance (or naivety) of their schemes.

Don't make them feel small.

Don't accuse them of childishness.

Don't react out of frustration; act from a plan.

Don't give money unconditionally for health purposes to an adult who's not taking care of himself. (Instead of spending $150 a month on the health insurance premium for someone who is spending $150 a month on cigarettes, can you make a Deal?)

Don't agree to support the adult child only to prove your love or trust or faith in them; do show those feelings directly, not with money.

> EXAMPLE: A man in his thirties brought his mother into family therapy because "she has done nothing but diminish me all my life." It turned out that he was enraged at her refusal to "lend" him more than a hundred thousand dollars for a business investment. "This is a test," he yelled at her in my office, after she had explained that her caution had nothing to do with her opinion of his ability. "Not trusting me proves you have *no* regard for my ability. How am I supposed to believe in myself if my mother doesn't even believe in me?"

This was obviously a man with problems, which would not have been solved by his mother giving in to his demands. (As he didn't return to therapy after I failed to take his side against her, I never learned whether his problems were treatable at all.)

My final and most important Don't: if your youth has an addiction, don't make the treatment/enabling bargain! The latter happens when a parent, spouse, or other family member, eager to get their loved one into treatment, promises an inducement of some kind that enables the addiction to continue. Counseling, rehab, support groups, psychiatry and/or medication should be rewarding in themselves, as the youth feels their positive effects. By all means, pay for the treatment—but only when they genuinely seek it for its direct benefits. If they're going along with it only to get something else from you, no program is likely to be effective. (Not even medication, because they won't stay on it unless they see its value.) If you have to bribe your youth to cooperate in a therapeutic program of any kind, he or she is manipulating you, merely maintaining the pipeline of funds that enable self-destructive habits to continue.

In fact, the same caution applies to treatment for other problems, not only addiction. When you're willing to provide something you believe is helpful to your child's growth, whether it's therapy or health insurance or a rent-free office, you're doing so because it is helpful in itself. It makes no sense to pay the individual an additional inducement to accept that help. In the case of therapy, he or she has a choice: either continue suffering from the anxiety disorder, ADD, drug problem or depression; or accept the offer of professional help. Making the wise choice shouldn't be a way to get extra money out of you. Reaping *the benefits of the treatment itself* will make them better able to earn, save, and spend responsibly.

VII. Banking 101: Budgets Don't Work

When money troubles rise to the level of a crisis that can't be ignored—when your Deal insists they not be ignored—young adults are ready to benefit from a parent's or coach's supervisory support. Sit down with them to go patiently through the steps of paying bills, assessing their cash flow, and looking at the trend over time.

This chapter looks at someone who has had trouble covering her regular expenses, but hasn't yet incurred significant debts. The next chapter, Banking 201, will extend the same bill-payment routines and coaching that we describe here, to the more difficult, yet common case where a credit card balance and other debts threaten to make the "simple" exercise of paying bills a hair-raising experience.

For *any* young person, tracking income and expenses is as much about time and attention as it is about money. Too *little* attention to the tedious or depressing matter of bill paying will soon make the situation worse, while *too much* attention to it interferes with the youth's natural Zen: to live in the moment. As we have seen, time and attention are big problems for many people, who instinctively react with avoidance. Yet those who write checks without keeping track of their balance, or postpone bill-paying because they fear looking at the bank balance, only make life more difficult for themselves.

Budgets don't work

Almost all authors on personal finance prescribe making a budget, which may be a good solution for disciplined people whose only problem is the modesty of their income. But few people actually live by budgets—least of all the money-disordered. Nick and I recommend a simpler method that provides the major benefits of a budget while being much less burdensome in practice.

Why isn't careful budgeting realistic for the young people we're writing about? Because they can't predict what they're going to need, or spend, beyond their regular monthly bills.

Instead, in this chapter, we'll describe how to help young adults use their bank statements—reports of what they actually spent—to show them where their bottom line is headed and to suggest remedies, both on the spending and the earning sides.

We want you to arrange to get together with your son or daughter, by phone if not in person, to walk them through paying bills in two sessions each month (so as not to miss any bill's due date). On one of those two occasions, you'll take ten or fifteen minutes to check the month's cash flow and discuss its trend over recent months.

You may be one of those people for whom bill-paying is merely a boring chore, not a mental challenge. If so, you wouldn't imagine some people need help, time after time, for months, until they master it. Yet that is what your learner may need—twice a month, even if only for moral support.

His or her checking account is more than a place to store and pay out money. It's your classroom. As you review the numbers together—with elementary arithmetic—the bank's monthly statements become your textbook about the impact of the learner's choices. At the same time, this session is your opportunity to instill confidence and self-esteem through implicit or explicit messages, "I'm here to help" and "we can do this."

Regular time

Let's set the scene for the exercise you're going to do, which will become a regular part of your relationship for a while. The financial picture it reveals may come as a relief, or it may be discouraging, initially. In either case, sticking to this routine will eventually lead to independence, as well as peace of mind. Both of you will be more secure, knowing that you're realistic about the situation (neither denying nor exaggerating a crisis). Your

Use your own system

Any system that works for *you* in paying bills, monitoring cash flow and avoiding bounced checks is what you'll probably teach to your learner, rather than exactly the system described here. If he or she uses online banking, you can do the twice-a-month checkups there, or consider EarnTrust™, which is designed for coach/learner pairs. This chapter's step-by-step, confidence-building paper-and-pencil process is merely an illustration of the fact that keeping track of basic numbers doesn't require many categories. Nor does a coach's help have to consume much time.

patience provides reassurance at the same time you're conveying knowledge. And you both see that your learner *can* improve the situation gradually.

Telling them, "Just go do it," is not the way. Don't let it become haphazard, or something you keep postponing. That sets the wrong example. Regular bill paying is obligatory.

Find a time when you're most likely to be together, if you live near enough, or a regular time to talk by phone. Maybe it's every other Sunday, or the first and third Tuesdays of each month at 10 PM. What I'll describe here is an in-person, computerless version of the exercise. You can add electronic bill paying and also do these sessions by long-distance telephone if necessary, both of you looking at the bank account online (see box, and Appendix). But the easiest way for me to convey the essential points is by imagining you side by side at a desk or table, with nothing but paper, checkbook, and a pen.

The first time you do this, you'll set up a couple of sheets to record monthly information, as I'll show you. Subsequent meetings will take as little as fifteen minutes, rarely more than thirty, including a cash flow update at one of those sessions and an update on debts in the other. Of course, you can reschedule for any reason, but do put the regular date on both your calendars, as a commitment. (Writing "To Do" tasks on the calendar is especially important if your son or daughter has ADD.)

Regular space

Your learner needs a designated place where she'll always sit to pay her bills. The kitchen table? Fine, but she needs to keep a folder for incoming bills, another (perhaps an accordion folder with alphabetic tabs) for paid bills, and other folders for bank statements and deposit slips, envelopes, and stamps—all in a nearby place. When a bill comes in, it goes in the folder. When it's paid, it goes in the paid folder. Don't let bills lie around in the open. Clients have told me they're afraid to put bills out of sight lest they forget to pay them, yet seeing them on the table or dresser provokes feelings of reproach, dread, and ultimately avoidance. The calendar is a much better reminder system! Any bill that isn't already overdue can safely wait in the folder from the day it arrives until your scheduled twice-a-month payment session.

Nick: Risk of relying on roommates

If you're coaching someone who doesn't live with you, make sure they have a failsafe system for putting stamped envelopes in the mail. A basket near the door where roommates leave outgoing mail to be dropped in the corner mailbox by whoever's going out? Cat knocks basket over. Envelope to bank with paycheck deposit sails under the refrigerator. Rent check bounces. Not good.

Say your son is sitting down to pay the bills. Does he have enough in the bank to pay all the current ones? Will there be enough in the next two weeks to live on and also pay the other bills that will have come due? If the answer to either question is no, you're there to advise on which ones have to be paid most urgently, and why. You're also there to discuss the pros and cons

---

The bank account

Open a checking account with a bank that has a "youth checking" or "student account":
- ✓ no minimum balance,
- ✓ low or no fees (forgo the negligible interest in favor of this),
- ✓ both of you listed on the account with distinct IDs and passwords.

They'll offer a credit card. Just say NO. If credit card debt isn't already part of the problem, this is no time to add it.
- ✓ Do get a debit/ATM card with a daily limit.
- ✓ Do take the option of receiving each month's cancelled checks, or a photocopy of all of them.
- ✓ Do make sure the bank offers online check paying. Even if you don't choose to use that feature now, one or both of you may, later.
- ✓ Find a bank that allows you and the learner to log on with different levels of privileges: for example, you might reserve to yourself the ability to change the ATM limit, or to sign up for such dubious "features" as "overdraft protection" (a back-door way of selling the unwary youth a high interest line of credit).

---

of borrowing or lifestyle changes. (We'll get to those in the following chapters.)

Step One: obligations, needs, and wants

Start by asking him to make a list on a clean sheet of paper, of everything that might affect his bank balance over the next two weeks. This would include all bills that are due, purchases he intends to make by check or debit card, any cash he'll need for daily needs, as well as any deposits he expects to be able to make. It will look something like this:

Item	Due	
phone	8/2	$42.33
rent	8/1	$435
jeans	?	Buy -- $60?
2 wks cash		$100?
deposit paycheck	8/1	about $460

Step Two: correcting the available balance

Now you need two pieces of information: the balance in his checking account *today*, which either of you can get online or at an ATM; and the amounts of all transactions not yet cleared. You probably know why that is necessary, but I'm going to go through it here, because some of the explanations I've found on bank websites or in their printed literature are too incoherent for many young people to absorb. They seem to assume everybody knows how checks are processed between banks. I would not assume that your son or daughter has that knowledge.

Deposits not yet cleared. Take a minute to explain that when you deposit a check from someone into your own account, your bank sends an inquiry to the bank on which that check was drawn: "A check for $___ has been presented to us from Account # _____ . Will you honor that check and transfer the money to us?" Until the confirmation comes back from the other bank (one or two business days, and the answer might be *no*), you can't use those funds. This is why your bank will only cash a check made out to you if you already have at least the same amount in your available balance.

Checks not yet cleared are those you have written that your bank doesn't yet know about. The payee may not have received it yet, or hasn't yet cashed or deposited it, or his bank may still be in the process of clearing it through the system to get the money out of your account.

Beyond paper and pen

Additional tools are available if you download the transactions into a desktop application such as Quicken®, which would give you more categorizing and report features, or into the web-based program www.EarnTrust.net. The latter allows learner and mentor to log on simultaneously from separate locations, and to project income and expense estimates into the future based on "what-ifs" such as buying a car, changing jobs, moving, or taking out a loan. (See Appendix.)

Even if you don't need those fancier programs, I suggest that you shop for a checking account at a bank whose website would let you export your transaction records in one of the formats that such programs can import. Thus you'll have that option available if you want it later, without having to change banks. The question to ask the banker is whether their online account page downloads data in financial format, such as QIF (Quicken™ Import Format) or .OFX (Open Financial eXchange). If all you can get are .txt (text) files or .xls (Excel™) spreadsheets, try a different bank.

Many people avoid the uncertainty—and penalties for writing a check with insufficient funds—by keeping a fat balance in their checking account. Young people can't always do that, unless they have accepted so-called "overdraft protection" on their account, authorizing their bank to honor checks beyond their available balance. Naturally, the bank charges a credit card rate of interest for that "feature"—an expensive remedy for anyone whose funds are tight.

Available balance (as reported by your bank) consists of only those deposits you made in cash, plus check deposits that cleared through the banking system, minus your payments that have cleared. However, the balance that truly reflects your solvency would be today's available balance *plus any deposits not yet cleared, minus any payments not yet cleared*. What the bank reports as available at this moment won't necessarily be available an hour from now, for payment purposes!

These problems never arise for those who pay for everything with cash or a debit card, but assuming your learner has a checkbook, there is no alternative to making a note of every deposit and every withdrawal by hand. Fortunately, one does not have to do the math each time (subtracting each check from a running balance on the check stubs, as we were taught back in the day), because you can check off the items that have already cleared the bank. A rough adjustment for deposits and payments not yet cleared, if any, tells you what is really available for new payments today.

	Day	Date	Dep	Pay	Balance
In bank today	Sunday	7/27			**$408**
Payments not yet cleared				58	**$350**
Deposits clearing		7/29	35		**$385**

This table will become our current action list. The first line is what the bank calls "available balance." We corrected it because we know we already wrote a $58 check that the bank may not find out about for days or weeks; but we can count on that $35 deposit we made at the ATM today being available by Tuesday.

Step Three: item list to action list

Now it's just a matter of spending the money available on items from the needs/wants list, in order of importance, never letting the balance go below zero. For example, that phone bill of $42.33 can be paid immediately, and there's no problem getting $100 in cash and even buying the jeans this week. Then, as our running balance shows, we need to deposit Friday's paycheck and wait until Monday for it to clear, before we pay the landlord:

	Day	Date	Dep	Pay	Balance
In bank today	Sunday	7/27			**$408**
Payments not yet cleared				58	**$350**
Deposits clearing		7/29	35		**$385**
Phone due 8/2	Monday	7/28		$42.33	**$343**
cash at Jewel	Monday	7/28		100	**$243**
jeans	Tuesday	7/29		60	**$183**
paycheck in	**Friday**	**8/1**	467		
paycheck clear	Monday	8/4			**$650**
Rent due 8/1	Monday	8/4		$435.00	**$215**
... etc					

Finally, we write the checks, put them in envelopes ready to mail, and cross them off when we mail them. (The phone bill is mailed today, but we'll pay the landlord in person on Monday). When everything on the action list has been crossed off, we can throw it away and just note that last number, $215, at the top of the next check stub. If the learner has occasion to write a check in the next couple of weeks (before doing this exercise again), he'll know what his true available balance was on August 4. Soon it becomes second nature to combine that fact with subsequent debits from the account, so as to have better knowledge of the true available balance at any time than the bank itself does.

An option is to go back and convert the original list of items to an action checklist:

~~Item~~ Action	~~Due~~ Do:	
Phone	Monday	$42.33 written, remember to mail
Rent	~~8/1~~ 8/4	check written, mail next Monday
jeans	~~2~~ OK	60 OK buy
Cash		$100 – OK up to $300
paycheck	8/1	deposit at bank on Friday

The leak in the bucket

Commonly, young people expect to earn enough, or get a sufficient allowance from parents, to pay their regular monthly bills with an amount left over that should be adequate for daily needs. But somehow, money in the form of checks or cash seems to leak out of the account. They buy food, household needs, entertainment, clothing … things that are just as important as the monthly bills. When those bills come in, there isn't enough in their account to pay them.

Read how Nick visualizes and controls the various demands for his monthly supply of money. Note his distinction between the regular monthly obligations and an irregular category that includes food, entertainment, and minor purchases. We're going to show a simple way of controlling the irregular spending, based on summary information from nothing more than the bank statements.

Nick: my overhead and my daily cash available
The single most helpful idea I've come up with—instead of monthly budgeting, which I found

96

useless—is thinking about my cash flow one day at a time. It's surprisingly easy to calculate.

First I see what amount of income I can basically count on, as a minimum every month. Last year, that was $3,000 before taxes. I made that much every month except one, which means I averaged more, but $3,000 was the amount I could spend in any calendar month without having to worry about it.

Next, I sum up the expenses that I'm going to have consistently: rent, phone, Internet, subway card, and now I've got an electric bill and health club. I add all those into one number, my monthly overhead before food. Of course food is even more necessary, but it's not a particular amount of money, nor is it like a bill that's going to be due. You can spend a lot on food—eating in restaurants or ordering in—or you can live on just a few dollars a day, buying ramen and fruit.

Therefore I group food along with other spending that's too much trouble to keep separate track of, yet easy to control if I use only cash.

I had learned to put aside $450 a month for the estimated taxes I had to pay every quarter, because I was self-employed. And my regular monthly bills at that time, rent and so forth, came to almost $1,500. So the income of $3,000, minus $450, minus $1,500 left me $1,050 a month that I could spend in cash or debit card without having to keep track of where it went, and without losing the roof over my head or having my phone or Internet canceled.

That works out to $35 a day. You have to figure out what's the best time interval for you, the way your mind and your life works. We're talking about skills, in this book, that have to be learned in the simplest personal way. It's not as much about math as it is about your own bizarre nature. For me, it was per day. I knew that any day I spent no more than my allowed average of $35, I wouldn't have to think about it.

The goal is to spend zero: eat the groceries you bought yesterday, let your Mom take you out to lunch. But if you buy something like a pair of jeans or some CDs that are going to take you over that cash limit, or if you go on a trip and spend $500, make sure you have previously accumulated that money in your bank account. You can say, I made $600 extra last month, so that's money I can spend over and above my $35 a day.

Similarly, if I got $35 from the ATM yesterday and still have some money in my pocket, I can take another $35 today and spend the total. It doesn't matter what I spend that amount of cash on.

I could get in trouble with cash very fast if I didn't know how much margin I had between my income and my overhead, but I didn't get in trouble as long as I knew how much that came out to per day and never went above it. Anything I wanted that I couldn't afford with my daily cash, I could only buy if I had the money from previously spending less, or I had a good month and got paid more, or my grandmother sent me a check for my birthday.

Hopefully, your overhead is always less than your income, or you'll starve. But when I figured out how much rent I could afford, I made sure I could meet my other monthly obligations with enough left over to eat.

I've progressed to taking my cash weekly, at the same time my earnings have risen faster than my overhead. So as long as I'm making my proven minimum monthly earnings, I have this marginal cash that I don't have to budget in categories. But if I started overspending again, I wouldn't hesitate to go back to the so-much-a-day method. People like me can't just go a whole month and then look back, "Let's see how much I have left over." We're not that type of person, as you know. The day that we are, we don't need this book. And it would make me crazy to keep track of where every dollar goes. What matters is not to go broke. This method prevents that; at least, until some unavoidable medical expense comes along. Which is one reason to gradually build up a savings account.

If your income permits, you can make "savings account deposit" one of your regular monthly obligations. I haven't managed to reach that point yet, probably because I live in New York City.

The shorter period of time you monitor yourself for, the faster you can detect when you're going out of control. This technique was a life saver for me because I only had to think about that one number, how much have I spent today? It allowed me to stay under my maximum every single day, and to let any remainder build up in my bank account. Bigger purchases have to be paid for by extra earnings or savings, rather than running over the daily max on routine stuff. Sure, if you plan to have a blowout weekend, you can set some cash aside in advance; but you can't do the opposite, spending next week's cash in advance. Keeping that mentality over time provides a cushion for someone who has my particular set of problems.

It's up to every individual person to know their own weakness. Everyone's going to have things that are and aren't a problem for them, mentally. It must come down to people's hard wiring. Some people have no trouble shopping for groceries and making their own meals, because they're extremely health conscious. As a matter of fact, when I stopped eating meat and learned to cook fish, eggs, and veggie dishes, I was amazed at how much I saved by cutting restaurant meals down to two or three a week.

If anyone asked me how to analyze their expenditures to figure out where the leaks in the bucket are, I'd say keep it simple: You know what you're most susceptible to as a consumer, because everyone knows. You don't need to keep track of every different category. You only need to know how much disposable cash you have.

The simple alternative to budgeting

As I've said, based on experience with Nick as well as many other young people, budgeting for things like food, entertainment, and so forth doesn't really work. The extreme version requires the learner to write down every penny he or she spends, in all the different categories, for a couple of months while working out the budget, and continue to do so thereafter. If you've ever tried that yourself, you scratched your head at the end of a day, trying to account for the missing $4.37, or you let a week go by and then couldn't begin to guess. There are people who have no problem with such an assignment, and might actually like it—but they are not the people we're trying to help!

The simpler system is to spend a few minutes once a month (for example, the first of your two bill-payment sessions), to get the basic facts from your monthly bank statements. Most of what a young person needs to track can be accomplished by breaking the income and expenses into two or three categories. You needn't make yourselves crazy.

We suggest you concentrate on the distinction Nick made in the illustration above, between the regular monthly bills and the irregular checks or cash that are impossible to budget.

The first step is to pull the gross numbers from each month's statement onto one ongoing record for the year. Suppose you're starting this exercise for the first time in July, but your daughter has had the bank account since February. Open the manila file folder where she keeps her bank statements, get a lined sheet of paper, and mark it with the four column headings shown below.

Total deposits and withdrawals for the month are shown somewhere on the statement: you don't have to total them yourselves. Go through as many months of history as you have since the last major change in her employment or living situation. In this example based on an actual twenty-two-year-old whom I'm calling Jill Jones, that would be February to June. (The February statement is the one whose *closing date* fell in February, and so forth.) Do this *with* her, double-checking that you've tabulated the correct numbers from each statement. In five minutes you'll have a chart something like this:

Charles Dickens said it memorably:

"My other piece of advice, Copperfield," said Mr. Micawber. "Annual income twenty pounds, annual expenditure sixpence under twenty pounds, result: happiness. Annual income twenty pounds, annual expenditure sixpence more than twenty pounds, result: misery."

(from *David Copperfield*)

Month	$$ In	$$ Out	Ending Balance
Feb	2,083	1,257	$831
Mar	1,515	1,332	$1,014
Apr	1,464	1,678	$500
May	1,298	1,418	$680
June	1,607	1,596	$691
July	1,242	1,535	$398

To an "Attention Money Disorder" sufferer (at any age), making charts like this is the treatment that brings relief. It's good to round to the nearest dollar, for this purpose. The fewer significant digits she has to look at, the better. You could even round to the nearest ten: $2,080, $1,520, $1,460, ...

When you have a chart with those past months filled in, you're ready to enter this month's numbers (July, in the table above).

At this point, you can see one important trend right away: Jill's monthly **Balance** is going down. In July it declined by $293, but on the average it's declined by about $87 a month: more than $400 since February.

If your real daughter's ending balances have held fairly steady month after month, and you see that she's keeping current with her bills and not accumulating any debts, you'll probably suggest she's ready to start handling her bills and bank account without you. Then your Deal no longer requires that you supervise your daughter in this area.

But Jill does need some help. Is the problem not enough earnings, too many monthly obligations, or too much irregular spending)?

Exploring the cash flow history

There's nothing like impersonal facts, in place of wishful projections. Often, as we'll see with Jill, the facts lead to constructive action.

She and her mother (the mentor in this case) want to know how much income she can count on, and how that compares with her spending. Her father has been contributing $500 a month toward Jill's rent. Their Deal was, he'd do that only for a year. When that subsidy ends, will she have to move back home?

It's easy enough to spot the paychecks among the deposits on Jill's bank statements: in July, for example, $500 was from Dad and the other $742 of deposits were paychecks.

So she and her mother go back to those monthly bank statements now, and split the deposits for each month into two columns. They make an **Earnings** column for the total of Jill's paychecks, month by month. It's easiest to use the month in which the deposit shows up on the bank statement, rather than the dates on her pay stubs. In February, only $738 of the money deposited in the account came from Jill's paychecks. In July, the bank statement showed two paychecks deposited, totaling $742. (Don't worry about the fact that checks aren't deposited precisely within every monthly cycle. Over the months, they'll average out to a meaningful picture.) Notice that the **$$In** numbers in the table above are the **Total** column here:

$$In

Month	Total		Take-home Earnings	Gifts & Loans
Feb	2,083	=	738 +	1,345
Mar	1,515	=	715 +	800
Apr	1,464	=	964 +	500
May	1,298	=	798 +	500
June	1,607	=	767 +	840
July	1,242	=	742 +	500

"**Gifts and Loans**" is everything besides earned income. Gifts of money go here, as do parental allowance, borrowed funds she put in the bank, transfers from a savings account or a trust fund—anything that isn't earned income. You don't have to list them and add them up, because the bank's statement shows total deposits each month and you'll just subtract the paychecks.

The repeated $500 in that column is her monthly allowance for rent, from the Deal with Dad. The additional amount in February came when Jill's lease ended and her former landlord returned her $845 security deposit. (She then moved to her friend Pam's apartment, who didn't ask for a deposit.) A surprise $300 check from her grandmother in March also helped, as did a $340 loan from Mom in June, when she had to buy a bridesmaid's dress for a wedding.

Unrecorded cash. You won't have a record of cash received (for example, from baby-sitting) that was never deposited in the bank. Therefore, whatever we wind up estimating that Jill can comfortably spend per week on unaccounted stuff—say,

$150—means $150 plus any extra, unbanked cash that comes her way.

In other words, for planning purposes we only care about *input* to the checking account and *withdrawals* from the checking account. If you and your learner really need to know the full story on her cash flow, she'll have to deposit all cash and checks in full, and then make any cash withdrawals. That would mean she couldn't ask the supermarket checkout clerk for cash back when using her debit card for groceries. Such rigidity is rarely worth the effort. (It's impractical to track the actual food portion anyway, with soap, beer, cigarettes, and flowers among the supermarket purchases.) In this system, we only care about the *difference* between deposited funds and withdrawn expenses. That number is the same whether Jill earned $900 and spent $700 or really earned $1,000 and spent $800.

Even before breaking down Jill's expenditures, the tables above are enough to see that the **$$In Take-home Earnings** column has supplied only about half of the **$$Out** amounts shown in the previous table. Jill can use a calculator to find averages (earnings averaged $787 per month while spending was $1,466), or just eyeball the range of numbers in each column: they aren't even close. She may have preferred not to be confronted with that news. The good news is, she's forced to be realistic. It's time to start analyzing, economizing, and job hunting.

$$Out categories. Now they'll look at each month's **$$Out** and break that down somewhat, without making themselves crazy. Even without assigning all the payee names to categories (as you'd do in a computer application), withdrawals from the account fall into three categories that are easy to identify from the bank statement: monthly checks, irregular checks, and cash.

Jill happens to know her regular monthly items:

Rent to Pam	$475
Share of utilities	varies around $60
Phone	varies around $45
Gym	$40
Student loan	$50
Total	**$670**

Her after-tax earnings of $787, minus those monthly costs, leave her $117, less than $4 a day to live on. Good luck! But we know that she actually spent an average of $1,466 total, so if $670 was the average for monthly bills, she was spending almost $800, or about $27 a day on the miscellaneous stuff. Is $27 a day extravagant? Maybe not, but Jill can't afford to keep that up, even with the temporary subsidy from her father, which will end next February. Unless she moves back home, or her parents plan to go on subsidizing her rent, she'll almost need to double her earnings by then.

Divide the cancelled checks (which you elected to have the bank mail back to you with each statement) into three piles. One pile are the monthly obligations: in Jill's case, rent and utilities, phone, and gym membership. Another pile are all other checks except those made out for cash. The third category consists of those checks written for cash, if any, plus everything she withdraws by debit card or ATM transactions (labeled on the bank statement).

The information here may be enough for the two of you to discuss where she can start trimming her expenses. Is the main problem regular monthly bills like rent and phone, or her irregular spending?

$$OUT

Month	total w/drawn	=	regular bills	+	irregular checks	+	cash w/drawn
Feb	1,257	=	615	+	412	+	230
Mar	1,332	=	769	+	368	+	195
Apr	1,678	=	754	+	774	+	150
May	1,418	=	612	+	581	+	225
June	1,596	=	603	+	763	+	230
July	1,535	=	671	+	637	+	227
Avg	**$1,439**		**$670**				

We have copied the total withdrawals from the bank statements to the first column of this sheet. Now you classify those into **regular bills, other checks,** and **cash**. The regular bills column contains all the contractual obligations, such as rent and utilities—the bills Jill has to pay once a month. We already know how much each of those bills comes to, so we don't need to list them out separately every month. If the whole category of obligations ($670 on average, in this example) turns out to be unsupportable, *then* look at the most recent monthly payments. She'll know whether it's the phone contract that could be reduced, or she's not getting to the gym enough to justify the membership, and whether the other monthly items are already as low as they can be.

She also basically knows the kinds of things she spends cash for. In this case, her **cash** column shows fairly small numbers because Jill prepares most of her own meals (and doesn't take cash back when she pays the supermarket by check). Her boyfriend funds much of their entertainment. So there probably isn't a need to analyze the cash further, in Jill's case.

There are some expense items you can't identify from the payee names on the checks. It won't be possible to total up cigarette costs, for example. Similarly, you're not going to be able to isolate food, laundry, concert tickets, or other irregular items bought in a variety of places, often for pocket cash. This is what I mean by not making yourselves crazy.

There happens to be a category in that **other checks** group, however, that Jill and her mother are curious about: how much is she spending on clothing? She likes to shop for clothes, but she tries to be economical about it. She feels like she's been spending no more than $150 a month on clothing, on the average. Her mother thinks it's more, and if so, it would account more than anything else for the continued decline in the bottom line. So this is a question worth further investigation.

They decide to go back through those checks in the **other checks** category and add up the ones to clothing stores. This becomes its own category, and now they lump all non-clothing irregular checks together with the cash as **other stuff**.

$$OUT

Month	total w/drawn	=	regular bills	+	clothes	+	other stuff
Feb	1,257	=	605	+	309	+	343
Mar	1,332	=	769	+	345	+	218
Apr	1,678	=	754	+	539	+	385
May	1,418	=	612	+	368	+	438
June	1,596	=	603	+	565	+	428
July	1,535	=	672	+	364	+	500
Avg	$1,439		$670		$415		$354

A minute with a calculator shows that the wardrobe purchases have averaged $415 a month, significantly more than Jill thought she was spending. And that doesn't count any clothing or accessories she may have paid cash for. If she wants to know *exactly* how much she's spending on clothes from now on, she can start saving all clothing receipts in an envelope on her bedroom dresser.

Is there another category to examine, after the wardrobe additions? You'll dig only as far as you think would be useful and controllable. Everything you don't create a special category for is still included in your forecast under **other stuff**. If you can't or don't choose to single it out for control, don't expect it to decrease in the future.

Sometimes **other stuff** will include an unusually large expense in one month, perhaps a computer purchase or a trip to Hawaii. You'll have to decide whether to ignore that item when averaging **other stuff** for forecasting purposes, because you don't expect it to be repeated in the foreseeable future. Still, there's always something, isn't there? Don't assume an expense was extraordinary unless it was *really* extraordinary. The down payment on a car, maybe. But if she suddenly had to cough up $800 for a transmission job, that may be the only one she'll have in a lifetime, yet it's not extraordinary; it's car maintenance.

Jill doesn't have a car. Another person might want to keep car expenses in their own column. They could save all gasoline receipts and repair bills in an envelope or folder, whether paid by check or cash, and enter them in the car column at the end of the month.

Our point is, *use only those categories that might help the young person make decisions.* Start with *as few categories as possible.* Only add more if they matter, and if you can realistically identify them each month by the payee on the check, the debit card statement, or saved receipts. Keep it simple: lump everything else into undifferentiated "stuff".

Even if you were to categorize every check, there would always be what Nick and I call the Cash Fog. As he said, it's almost impossible to track where cash goes. Furthermore, Jill may not

Opportunity costs

Another youth writes few checks other than his regular monthly bills, but spends four times as much cash as in the Jill example. Why? Because he doesn't buy groceries. He eats out, or orders in, a couple of times a day. Ask him to estimate what the equivalent number of calories would cost if purchased in the form of cans, raw meat or fish, and fresh produce. Does he realize that one restaurant meal could buy groceries for at least five meals he could prepare for himself, or that coffee at Starbucks costs about ten times as much as at home? This is the sort of discussion that joint review of the checking account data will stimulate.

Any major purchase involves opportunity costs. Difference between a new and used car could be as much as $600 a month (payments and operating costs of $800 for the new car, versus $200 for the used). "It's *worth* $600 to me," the youth says. But is it worth $7,200 a year? That's enough to furnish a whole apartment *and* make all your student loan payments for the year. The same logic applies to the difference between a $1,400 apartment shared with one roommate ($700 a month, each) and a $1,600 one shared with three others ($400 a month). That's $3,600 in a year. The question shouldn't be, "Does it *feel like* it's worth that much to you, subjectively?" but "What else could that money do for you at this stage in your long life?"

care to disclose all her cash purchases. She may have paid for one or two things you don't need to know about.[17] Leave her to draw the conclusion about their impact on her bottom line. The point of this is not to be a detective or an auditor, it's to help *her* get basic numbers in order and learn how to keep them that way.

---

17   Your purpose is neither to snoop nor to control the young person, it's only to mentor her in taking charge of her money. This system is most likely to lead her eventually to draw mature conclusions about those recreational purchases, if they affect her bottom line either directly or indirectly. On the other hand, if recreation becomes addiction, it will become clear. It will not happen because you "neglected" to get truthful information about her cash expenses.

"How do I convince my kid to do this?"

It's understandable that many young people, probably a majority of them, will say "no, thanks," when a parent offers to do this kind of coaching on a regular schedule. They may be embarrassed or distressed to be confronted with the reality of their economics. They won't recognize that the payoff to them, relative to the small amount of time required of them, beats their hourly wage. And it won't occur to them that your offer to spend this time helping them is a gift.

If you're wondering what to say when they decline your offer, you must have skipped or forgotten Chapter II. This is part of your Deal! You're subsidizing the young person (or someone is), and you *require* them to accept this mentoring as a condition of maintaining that subsidy.

Numbers are our friends

That's all you need to do, until the picture gets more complicated with debts. We've added an hour a month to time you're going to spend in person or on the phone with your child—longer the first time, but thereafter about thirty minutes, twice a month. You might not have considered this as quality time, but that's what it is. Just try it, remembering our Dos and Don'ts from Chapter VI!

Take the time to show your learner how neatly the tables in these exercises add up to the whole story.

- Each month's ending balance is the previous balance plus deposits, minus withdrawals.

- Deposits include earnings, gifts, and loans.

- Expenses include certain fixed expenses that we can only control by cancelling or changing features in a contract, plus checks we write for discretionary purchases, plus borrowed money we repay, plus a fog of cash that's virtually impossible to control unless we limit our withdrawals of cash from the bank.

All of this is knowable, trackable, plannable, manageable. It may seem elementary to you. But this is basically what she didn't get before. It's a good feeling to see one's own numbers match the bank's, and to understand why they do.

Nick's daily limit for spending that he doesn't have to keep track of (sure earnings minus overhead, divided by thirty) may or may not be a helpful technique for your son or daughter. As he said, "It's not as much about math as it is about your own bizarre nature." Let them try their own ways of envisioning the supply and demand for their money, while you continue supportively joining them twice a month to pay the bills, adding a new row to those **$$In** and **$$Out** tables with each monthly statement.[18] The tables soon make this youth's situation vividly apparent to both of you.

We'll discuss the problem of debt thoroughly in the next three chapters. Here I want to emphasize that this moment, when you've paid her bills (if possible) and are looking at her bank balance and its trend over time, is what educators call a "teachable moment." It's an ideal occasion to discuss what Jill still needs to work on. You've just helped her see, in a concrete, objective way, the reality of her situation. You're not moralizing or sermonizing, merely making her see her situation realistically. Her goal is to build up a positive cash flow so she can pay not only her bills, but any debts she has, and anything she wants to save toward.

Action planning

Of concern to Jill in this example is the fact that her earnings are flat, and the monthly take home average of $787 doesn't cover

---

18   Since you probably need to have two sessions each month for regular bill paying, you might use one of those for reconciling the bank statement and updating $$In and $$Out, and use the other bill paying session to update the Debt balance and review the future outlook.

her basic living costs. Dad's subsidy is good only through next January. So, what can she do about the excess of spending over income? Will her job allow her to add more hours? Is it time to get serious about looking for a better job? Or is there room to trim her expenses?

Suppose Jill is riding public transportation to work every day. Good! But it's a long trip with two transfers, two and a half hours out of her day, five times a week. A car would give her more hours in which to work, including some evenings instead of all day shifts (bigger tips). Unfortunately, right now, she can't afford a car. Her mother can spare her car four evenings a week. But Jill would have to buy the gas.

They've calculated that she'd need an extra $120 a month for gas, and they think she'd probably make $400 more per month, after taxes, with night shifts. So this would help reduce the deficit between her expenses and her income, by $280. That would put her in the black, but only until Dad's rent Deal runs out. She's still not covering that $500.

Add a second, part-time job? Get a job in her own neighborhood, and work more hours?

Or cut back on expenses? What about that clothing category? Counting the bridesmaid's dress she had to buy (probably not the last), Jill's wardrobe additions averaged $415 per month. She and Mom can now talk about that: can she cut that in half?

Then there are those monthly bills. Is she *using* the gym membership? As you see, it isn't necessary to sort all types of expenditure into a lot of specific categories. Jill knows fairly well what the components are; she may not know the exact numbers, but she knows the items she could cut down on. That is what matters. Or maybe you both agree that her expenditures *aren't* excessive, it's a matter of getting more aggressive about searching for that better job.

We've been talking about what Jill herself needs to do. How can her parents help, whether divorced like Jill's, or acting together?

What would I do if she were my daughter? I might offer to cover the rent for a second year, as long as she stabilizes her bank balance and begins to build it. Alternatively, if she does need to move back home and that's acceptable to me, I'd make her feel welcome and try my best to treat her as a responsible adult housemate, not the teenager she was when last in residence. We both need to accept non-judgmentally the fact that she, like many others her age, can't yet afford her own place.

And what about taxes?

In this example—difficult enough as it is—we haven't considered taxes. That's because Jill's employer withheld tax and FICA from her paycheck. She doesn't have to worry about finding the money to pay taxes when filing time comes. Assuming she declared zero dependents on the form she filled out with Personnel, the amount withheld will probably cover the taxes due on those earnings, and she may even get a welcome refund.

Many people, like Nick, work on an independent basis: from day laborers to nannies to computer consultants. An employer who pays them by check is almost certainly declaring that expense and reporting the taxable payment (if $600 or more in a year) and the payee's social security number to the Internal Revenue Service. Woe to the payee who's caught failing to report the income.

Suppose you're trying to help your youth file accurate tax returns, paying tax due on the earned income, but the money's been spent already![19] To avoid that painful situation, Nick found the simplest method was to have a place separate from the checking account—it could be a savings account at the same bank—where he immediately sequestered 15 percent of his taxable paychecks. You might adjust the percentage after a year or two of experience, but the idea isn't to have *exactly* the right amount of money there.

---

19   Get a tax accountant or preparer to advise you on whether you need to pay quarterly estimated tax, and how to set that up. Our concern here is only to ensure that the money's been set aside for payment whenever due.

Forgo interest; go for the lowest fees

We've been talking here about a *checking* account. Most banks offer simple accounts designed for young people. Wooing young customers in hopes of keeping them when they get more money, the banks either waive fees entirely (up to a certain number of checks per month) or offer an account with very low fees and no minimum balance. With your own checking account, you may have opted for a $1,000 minimum balance that gets you free checking and maybe even a little interest thrown in. You don't mind the $1,000 requirement, because you're more comfortable anyway keeping a cushion there. (You lose only $20 a year by not putting that $1,000 in a 2 percent savings account.) But your kids might have trouble keeping a $1,000 balance. They shouldn't have to pay a penalty, so long as they're not bouncing checks.

If your youth is accumulating actual *savings* (or already has inherited funds), you can help her build those in a savings or investment account that (a) gives the best return available while (b) allowing withdrawal when needed. (Locking a twelve-month or eighteen-month rate on a certificate of deposit might be fine if saving for college, but a problem if she needs money sooner to purchase a vehicle or lease an apartment.)

It's to teach the fact that this isn't spendable dough: the government will demand its share, and we want to avoid the penalties and interest they'll slap on us if we can't come up with that tax payment when it's due.

You'll need to keep a register like this:

	Earnings from which nothing was withheld	Transferred to savings	Cumulative balance
February	$870	15 % = $131	$131
March	$920	15 % = $138	$269
April	$795	15 % = $119	$388
… etc.			

The young taxpayer, or the two of you together, can do this each month when you balance the checking account statement. If he wants to move *more* than the tax reserve amount into his savings account, more is fine—but no less!

Savings accounts are fine for setting aside money that might be needed in the near future for taxes, or for a couple of months' living expenses in case of a sudden job loss. Once young people are consistently raking in more than they spend, and start thinking about some serious saving for future needs like houses, weddings, babies ("the whole catastrophe"), there are prudent ways to get much better returns than a low-interest savings account. But a savings account is a convenient place to set just enough money aside—away from that "available" checking balance—so those quarterly or annual income tax payments are never a crisis.

If your learner prefers to deposit 100% of pre-tax earnings in the checking account without setting anything aside, then the accrued tax obligation should be counted as a *debt*, as I'll show in the next chapter.

The bottom line

It's easy to help someone develop reliable, relatively stress-free bill-paying habits and the habit of thinking in terms of cash flow. You just set up a regular place to store and pay bills, and a couple of calendar dates for doing it.

Confronting choices about which bills to pay when money is short forces young people to realize the consequences of actions already taken. Those aren't consequences that can be avoided; the only choices available at this moment are about timing. Avoiding the task only makes it harder. However, the parent or coach need not, and should not, lecture or preach sermons about those bills at this point. Let the facts speak for themselves.

There is also much to be learned from a series of monthly bank statements, looking at little more than the monthly sum of deposits, sum of withdrawals, and one or two subcategories of each of those. Tabulating the pattern of earning and spending over many months reveals where one has choices about future income or spending, and how much of a difference alternative choices can make.

You will adapt our process to your learner's situation, of course, but in general these are the steps in your twice-a-month sessions:

1. Ascertain the money available in their checking account, today, and list any deposits expected in the next couple of weeks.
2. List all the bills that are due, or will be due in the next couple of weeks.
3. Write checks for those bills in order of importance, within the limit of money available; show a running balance over the next couple of weeks, as money goes in and out of the account.
4. Look at the money in and out over the past six months or so: has the balance been relatively stable, or is more flowing out than coming in?
5. If there's a negative cash flow, break the deposits down into earnings versus unearned deposits such as gifts, loans, or windfalls unlikely to be repeated. Can he or she count on anything more than after-tax earnings? Break the payments down into regular monthly items, irregular purchases you can identify, and unaccounted-for cash. Each of those is a potential area to look at in more detail, if necessary.

Keep it simple. The more you convey confidence that the two of you can solve any problems you discover (even if that means looking for better-paying work, taking on more hours at the existing job, or making a steep cut in expenses), the better this exercise will deliver the magic triad of parental gifts: Motivate, Teach, and Support.

VIII. Banking 201: Credit and Borrowing

In Chapter VII, we tabulated a learner's recent history of income and expenses, confronting reality while focusing on constructive behavior rather than past mistakes. In a similar way, once a month we insist on updating a log of current debts. The example here is a more serious crisis than the one in the previous chapter, but offers a silver lining: crisis produces the opportunity for a new Deal that motivates, teaches, and supports.

Jack's situation is more complicated and worrisome than the example in Chapter VII. A twenty-five-year-old musician, he teaches guitar and piano, works half time in a guitar shop, and earns a little cash on the side, every few weeks, with a jazz quintet. His parents thought he was getting by on those income sources, but with a car, a girlfriend 100 miles away, and a growing collection of instruments, he couldn't cover the rent on his loft apartment.

Although Jack would like to renew his lease, he is facing the fact that he is broke, and needs parental EMT: Emergency Money Treatment. He also has an invitation to move into a cheaper one-bedroom apartment, sharing the rent with his younger brother. He already owes his parents $400. He owes his girlfriend, Anne, $600. He has a small monthly car payment and a moderate student loan payment, but the big problem his parents only just learned about is a growing MasterCard balance.

Jack and his father begin by tabulating his last seven months' deposits and withdrawals, as we did in Chapter VII. The situation looks stable, as their table on the next page shows.

Month	$$ In	$$ Out	Ending Balance
Jan	1,378	1,338	$40
Feb	1,453	1,399	$94
Mar	1,353	1,382	$65
Apr	1,403	1,368	$100
May	1,378	1,372	$106
June	1,378	1,446	$38
July	1,453	1,384	$107

Apparently, Jack has managed to maintain a small balance in his checking account, even with an $800 rent payment. He will save $400 per month if he moves with his brother. His other monthly bills averaged just over $400, including the car and student loans, and his MasterCard minimum payment. Dad does the math with him, and it looks like he must have lived on an average of $186 in other withdrawals from the bank each month since January 1:

Month	total $$Out	=	regular bills	+	other $$Out
Jan	1,338	=	1,195	+	143
Feb	1,399	=	1,195	+	204
Mar	1,382	=	1,207	+	175
Apr	1,368	=	1,198	+	170
May	1,372	=	1,189	+	183
June	1,446	=	1,197	+	249
July	1,384	=	1,204	+	180
average	$1,384	=	$1,198	+	$186

That's $6.20 a day, for food, toiletries, gas and car repairs, going out with friends, laundry, ...? Something is wrong with this picture. Jack must have another source of funds.

The monthly debt table

In Chapter VII, we said that on one of your two dates each month to help or lend moral support to your kid's bill paying, the two of you will check over his bank summaries, as Jack and his father just did. Also once each month, if he or she has any debts (other than those with fixed monthly payments included in their regular monthly checks), you'll update a separate table like this:

	Jack's	Debts		
Month	Master Card	Owe Mom	Owe Anne	Total Debts
Jan	941	300		$1,241
Feb	955	300		$1,255
Mar	1,096	300		$1,396
Apr	1,113	400		$1,513
May	1,313	400		$1,713
June	1,507	400	600	$2,557
July	1,567	400	600	$2,567

Why no columns for Jack's car loan and student loan? Because they're already in his monthly bills. Their payment over time is accounted for. Loans of the latter kind, including mortgages, are secured by assets that the lender can repossess.[20] Unlike those

---

20   Is a student loan secured? You bet it is – see Chapter IX.

obligations, the debts in this table don't go away until one makes discretionary payments.

The MasterCard's *minimum* payment was included among the monthly bills, but as the word implies, that payment has a minimal effect on the numbers shown here, which Jack and his father copy from the credit card's monthly statements. Notice that his debt to MasterCard increased by $626 since the end of January, which answers the question of how Jack managed to spend only $6.20 per day beyond his regular monthly obligations: he didn't. He put more than $600 of charges on his credit card, and also borrowed $100 from Mom in April and $600 from his girlfriend in June.

Jack's work as a music teacher is self-employment income, unlike his job in the store, which withholds income tax and FICA from his paycheck. His parents taught him the wisdom of putting aside about 15 percent of his self-employment earnings each month in a savings account so he'll have enough to pay his taxes. (More on this in Chapter XII.) As long as the savings account is building up in rough proportion to the accruing tax obligation, they balance each other as an asset and a liability, so that obligation needn't be included here.

Your Debts table will include columns for all "unsecured" loans: money the youth owes you, other family members, friends, credit card companies, and any other loans that aren't on a monthly amortization schedule (paying off principal as well as interest).

Jack and has father review his unsecured loans, based on the credit card statement and Jack's own report of what he owes Anne. (This is not a government audit, it is a coaching exercise. The more accurately Jack reports his debts, the more helpful the exercise.)

It's not essential to reconstruct what his debts were in previous months. I did so in this example to resolve the mystery of Jack's subsistence on $6.20 a day. The first time you do this, you only need to know the accurate *current* debts, so you can bring them up to date from now on. One of you will keep this sheet in the folder with his bank statements where you can pull it out to update it, and discuss it, at least once a month. Your learner may have repaid some debts, in whole or in part, since last month. Or he may have borrowed additional funds from others. So it's helpful to make one column for each lender as shown above, ask how each account stands this month, and add the new row.

Jack reports the status of his debts. The bottom row shows the month's current balance for each loan, and the total amount of debt. These numbers have no direct connection with the bank account. For example, he incurred the debt to Anne when they charged expenses on her credit card. He might end up paying her back with cash from selling one of his guitars, or by cash from a jazz gig that never goes through his bank.

From problem to solution

Now they compare Jack's liquid assets and liabilities. Dad puts the Bank Balance table and Debt table side by side, with new rows after July to show the months ahead, in pencil. First, they assume his earnings and spending won't change, so he has to continue borrowing $221 per month. (His total debt increased by $1,326 over the past six months.) Assuming he uses his credit card for that, he would actually incur additional interest charges and have to raise his minimum payments, but Dad keeps it simple for purposes of this rough forecast. He simply adds $221 to the expected MasterCard balance each month.

	$$ In	$$ Out	Bank balance	Master Card	Mom	Anne	Assets minus debts
July	1,453	1,384	**$107**	1,567	400	600	-$2,460
Aug	1,400	1,400	**$107**	1,788	400	600	-$2,681
Sep	1,400	1,400	**$107**	2,009	400	600	-$2,902
Oct	1,400	1,400	**$107**	2,230	400	600	-$3,123
Nov	1,400	1,400	**$107**	2,451	400	600	-$3,344
Dec	1,400	1,400	**$107**	2,672	400	600	-$3,565

The right-hand column, comparing Jack's money with his debts, month by month, is similar to a business's net worth: Assets minus Liabilities. The difference is that we're not concerned with a youth's other assets outside of his bank account. What matters for our purposes is only the trend of his *bank account* and his *debts*. In Jack's case, those numbers are negative (note the minus signs), and growing more so.

Now – the good part

What's the point? To rub Jack's nose in the fact that by Christmas, he'll be in the hole to the tune of ten weeks' income? No: the purpose of this exercise is to look at his options. In this case, Jack's parents have not offered to subsidize his monthly shortfall, because they think it's high time for him to deal with the economic realities of his situation. Hence he is moving to a shared apartment, saving $400 in rent. He spent that amount this month on moving expenses, but beginning in August, if he makes no change in his spending habits, his bank balance could grow by $400 per month:

	$$ In	$$ Out	Bank balance	Master Card	Mom	Anne	Assets minus debts
July	1,453	1,384	**$107**	1,567	400	600	-$2,460
Aug	1,400	~~$1,400~~ $1,000	~~$107~~ **$507**	1,788	400	600	~~-$2,681~~ -$2,281
Sep	1,400	~~$1,400~~ $1,000	~~$107~~ **$907**	2,009	400	600	~~-$2,902~~ -$2,102
Oct	1,400	~~$1,400~~ $1,000	~~$107~~ **$1,307**	2,230	400	600	~~-$3,123~~ -$1,923
Nov	1,400	~~$1,400~~ $1,000	~~$107~~ **$1,707**	2,451	400	600	~~-$3,344~~ -$1,744
Dec	1,400	~~$1,400~~ $1,000	~~$107~~ **$2,107**	2,672	400	600	~~-$3,565~~ -$1,565

All Dad did here was reduce the money spent each month from $1,400 to $1,000, recalculate the running bank balance, and recalculate the net balance. (He knows how to subtract without a calculator.)

Jack would prefer to pay back his girlfriend and get the credit card debt down, rather than accumulate the money in his checking account. If he gives Anne $400 in August and $200 in September, then stops charging on the credit card and pays it off as soon as he can, how long do you guess that will take? It takes multiple calculations to work out on paper, but is easy with a computer spreadsheet. I can tell you (trust me) that by year's end Jack still owes Mom, but has paid the MasterCard down to zero and can use it to buy Christmas gifts for Mom, Anne, and his brother.

Obviously, your particulars will be different. But like Jack and his father, sitting down together and tabulating bank deposits and withdrawals, money owed and bank balance each month, leads you and your son or daughter to discuss constructive, realistic options.

The bottom line

You are beginning to see how the three principal components of our system work together: the Deal (Chapter II), the jointly monitored checking account (Chapter VII), parental rescue and debt relief (treated more fully in Chapter X). The Deal gives you the leverage to insist that your youth accepts your help tracking money in and out of the bank account as well as curtailing credit card and other debts. Conversely, looking at the bank balance and drawing information from the monthly statement confirms the Deal's expectations about bill payment, earnings, and debt.

Is there a Banking 301? Of course. The next level involves a computer: either a spreadsheet such as Excel™, dedicated software such as Quicken™, or a website like www.EarnTrust.net™. In addition to tracking many more categories, those tools help you graph the trends over time. You may decide, after all, to use more categories in examining every dollar earned and every dollar spent, for a few months. But try the simple paper and pencil exercises I've outlined, first. You might find they're all it takes to nudge your Jack, or Jill, onto the path of solvency.

IX. Inoculating Them Against the Epidemic

As a society, we're way over our heads in debt. Our media sound the alarm about this fact, but they're also to blame for promoting it, because lenders and merchants with "E-Z Credit" are big advertisers. There's no profit in advertising the pitfalls of "buy now, pay later." Young adults are particularly vulnerable to the temptations. It's up to us to teach them the difference between wise borrowing and dumb borrowing.

This chapter lays out some essential things American youth need to understand about debt, expressed in ways they can understand and use. For each topic, we emphasize the context for teaching it: at what ages (beginning before adolescence) and how to integrate motivation and support into your teaching.

We've been talking about falling into financial trouble as though it's a problem in young people. To a considerable degree, though, they're suffering from an endemic disease in twenty-first-century American society, at least as much as they are from naiveté and carelessness. Therefore, this chapter will make the case for inoculating our children against the economy's attempts to seduce them into debt. And we'll include some advice about younger children, in hopes of keeping them out of the straits your oldest may already be in.

America's endemic disease

An annual Survey of Consumer Finances administered by the Federal Reserve Board shows that U.S. families saved about 9 percent of their after-tax income from the 1950s through the mid-1980s.[21] That annual savings rate steadily declined during the 1990s, averaging around 2 percent between 1999 and 2004, then became *negative* in 2005. To put this in dollar terms, for

---

21   The government calculation counts savings deposits, investments, home improvements, and the pay-down of principal on their mortgage.

every $10,000 of after-tax earnings, the average family in the 1970s put about $900 into their home equity, savings account, or investments. By the turn of the century this was down to $200 per $10,000 of disposable income, and then became negative: for the first time since the Great Depression, by 2005 the average American family was accumulating more debt than savings.

Elsewhere in the world, poverty has many causes. In America, arguably the biggest cause of poverty is the debt industry: primarily, consumer lenders.

An old business adage is "go where the money is." But the banking industry built its most profitable, 30 billion dollar segment over the past two decades by recognizing that there was even more money to be extracted from those who have little, but who naturally desire a share in the material comforts they see around them. Sure, a bank can make larger loans to the rich, but there's a much bigger pool of those needing small loans, from a $100,000 mortgage down to a $1,000 medical bill or a $100 paycheck advance. And because they don't have much collateral with which to guarantee their loans, and may not have a good credit history, they expect to pay interest rates that the rich would never consider.[22]

On the day I'm writing this, a bank would get an average annual interest of about 7.5 percent from its loans to business owners and other wealthy customers. All of whom can easily pay that rate, out of the much higher returns they earn from their investments. The bank pays only 5 percent to borrow the money from central banks, but it also has to pay salaries, rent, and advertising expenses. So the profits from that group of borrowers are limited.

---

22   An excellent brief history of how the banking industry pulled this off is the article "The Ascendance of the Credit Card Industry" by journalist Robin Stein, on the PBS website: http://www.pbs.org/wgbh/pages/front-line/shows/credit/more/rise.html A good resource for protecting oneself against the companies' tactics is www.bcsalliance.com.

In contrast, a credit card holder who's making minimum payments—or even better, from the lenders' point of view, a twenty-five-year-old walking into a storefront loan office—pays interest at 18 percent to 30 percent. They do so not because they're suckers, but because they're poor. In fact, the poorer they are, the more interest they're charged. They want to buy a home? Offer them a balloon mortgage. When the payments balloon in a few years, by then (the lender encourages them to believe) they'll surely be earning more money, or the value of their home will have increased so they can refinance it at a lower rate.[23]

Which borrowers, then, will lenders go after most aggressively? The relatively few rich, at 5 to 10 percent interest, or the many needy, at 18 to 30 percent? The *neediest* turn out to be where the money is.[24]

The net result for those folks isn't to give them their piece of the American dream. On the contrary, in many cases, their loans turn into nightmares for them and their children.

Those of us who are middle aged and were fortunate in our educations and our earning capacity (or our inheritance) only learn about what it means to have a home mortgage foreclosed, or an automobile or furniture repossessed, from reading about such traumas or seeing them on television. But if we take a moment to look at the statistics, we realize that it's a fact of life for a great number of American families. According to the wholesale

---

23   As this goes to press, we have already seen the near collapse of America's, and as a consequence the global economy as a result of these practices. The predatory mortgage practices discussed here are over, for now at least. Nonetheless, it is important that we all understand how they got us here, and watch for their reincarnation.

24   Citigroup's balance sheet at the end of September 2008 showed a net worth of $99 billion. The line for its credit card companies showed $117 billion, net (the sum of everyone's outstanding balance on that day, less those companies' debts). In other words, all its businesses other than consumer credit were in the red. On November 14, Citi announced 20,000 job layoffs and its intention to raise interest rates on many of its credit cards by up to 3%.

vehicle auctioneer Manheim Consulting, 1.5 million cars and trucks were repossessed in the U.S. in 2007. And in the record home foreclosure year of 2008, close to a million families will have been forced to abandon their investment in their homes.[25]

The enormous growth in personal debt over the past twenty years in the U.S. isn't merely due to aggressive marketing by the credit industry. It is a direct result of change in our country's economic position relative to the rest of the world. We have had a huge deficit in exports (wheat, lumber, movies) relative to our imports (automobiles, electronics, oil). This means that our main export is now the money used to pay for our negative balance of trade. The foreign nations that sold us those consumer products, high-tech machinery, and natural resources invested much of the money we paid them right back into our economy—fortunately. But that influx of capital demanded to be put to profitable use, so Americans were encouraged to keep borrowing, and keep spending borrowed money on foreign goods, which in turn accelerated the trade deficit.

Economists don't agree as to whether all this means we're on the brink of the dollar's collapse (though it has certainly declined as never before in our lifetimes). Some say we're moving toward a more sustainable position in the global economy. I'm not an economist. My expertise is in human development and family relationships, so what concerns me is how all this debt undermines the maturation of so many of our young people.

A tough economy for the young

College graduates in the first decade of this century faced the worst job market in twenty years. Increased productivity due to technology has reduced the number of office jobs, while at the

---

25   Extrapolated on data through August from RealTrac, Inc. The Associated Press, Sept. 12, 2008. After the September financial meltdown, as this book was going to press, guesstimates in the media were ranging up to five times that number.

same time other countries have been acquiring technology that attracts American companies to shift jobs overseas.

Combine that fact with the greatly increased costs of U.S. higher education and the material comforts our youth have learned to expect, and they're in trouble. No wonder between 100,000 and 200,000 people below the age of twenty-five declare bankruptcy every year.[26] This despite all the best advice to those with serious debt, that bankruptcy should be the absolutely last resort. It's safe to assume that these 100,000 or 200,000 young people are only the tip of a gigantic iceberg. A much greater number averted bankruptcy by "consolidating" debt: a misnomer. Consolidating really means they spread it further into the future, trapping them in long-term, even lifelong debt: not quite drowning, yet with their nostrils barely above water and their toes groping in vain for the bottom.

Bankruptcies are of little concern to the lenders, because the fraction of borrowers who default are more than made up by the interest rates everyone else pays. Furthermore, the lending institutions know that the risk of default is low among the youngest group of debtors, because in most cases their parents will wind up bailing them out before allowing them to endure the stigma of "bad credit."

We can't expect the credit card companies to stop soliciting those hapless young people. Nor is it the government's job to decide who should be allowed to borrow in a free market (nor to bail out the borrower who defaults; nor his lender). Unquestionably, the only solution is to educate young people, from an early age, about the difference between wise borrowing and dumb borrowing.

---

26 Report of the 2001 Consumer Bankruptcy Project, Harvard and New York University Law Schools and the Ford Foundation. The number of bankruptcy filings at all ages was around 1,500,000 per year.

Wise versus dumb borrowing

Is there such a thing as wise borrowing? Yes. It's wise to borrow capital for business investments that one has reason to believe will bring a better return than the cost of borrowing. It can also be wise to borrow for a home mortgage—taking account of the fact that your home holds its value while you're living in it[27], unlike vehicles, electronics, vacations, clothing, which often are used up before one is done paying for them. Even for those expenditures, however, borrowing can be smart any time the cost is more significant to you today than it will be in the future.

Nick: smart borrowing

You want an example? Tickets for a concert are going on sale this Friday, and they'll be sold out before I get paid next Friday. Will you lend me $50 so I can buy the ticket, and I'll pay you $51 next week? If you trust me, sure you will; you'll be earning an annual return of 104 percent (2 percent per week). Yet paying the extra dollar is a good deal for me, because I'd have to pay $150 on the street for those tickets if I wait until the day of the show.

The definition of wise borrowing is *not*, as many supposed experts say, "establish good credit by making your payments reliably." We define it as *only taking on debt for purchases that will increase your earning capacity, or save you money in the long run, or build your equity in an appreciating asset.*

A common example of *un*wise borrowing is when a business owner takes out a home equity loan in order to shore up a failing business. Even more common, and dumber, is when a consumer borrows more than he or she has a reasonable expectation of being able to repay.

---

27   Median U.S. home values rose every year from 1932 through 2007. Not so in 2008.

The dumbest borrowing is the kind that's all too common among young adults: when their credit card is maxed out or their income is insufficient to make payments on it, they take out another card.

A survey by the Jump$tart Coalition for Personal Financial Literacy found that one in six U.S. *twelfth-graders* use a credit card in their own name. Among college undergraduates, student loan company Nellie Mae found that students add one credit card after another, increasing to *four or more* for a majority of college seniors (see box). Yet, anyone who has more than one credit card is digging a deeper hole with every purchase. There was a reason the first credit card had a limit!

An Indiana University administrator was quoted as saying that his school had more students dropping out due to credit card debt than to academic failure.[28]

Such statistics and his own research led Robert D. Manning, professor at Rochester Institute of Technology, to say in testimony to Congress: "The unrestricted marketing of credit cards on college campuses is so aggressive that it now poses a greater threat than alcohol or sexually transmitted diseases."[29]

How our economy sucks young people into unwise debt

Although some leading economists have long predicted that our love affair with borrowing would bring down the whole U.S. economy[30], what concerns me here is how this trend feeds upon our youth. I see it doing so in three ways: by creating false expectations; by exploiting their ignorance; and by charging exorbitant interest rates and fees.

Expectations. Advertisers and the media (which must serve advertisers, to survive) all create and foster a culture in which one's identity depends on how much one spends. The best way

---

28   Godfrey, Neale. *Money Still Doesn't Grow on Trees*. Rodale Press, 2004, p. 123.

29   See Manning's website www.creditcardnation.com and *Credit Card Nation: America's Dangerous Addiction to Consumer Credit*. Basic Books, 2001.

30   Kevin Phillips, *American Theocracy*. Penguin, 2007.

A survey of college credit card usage in the U.S.

Seventy-six percent of undergraduates began the school year with credit cards.

The average outstanding balance on undergraduate credit cards was $2,169.

As students progress through school, credit card usage swells. Forty-two percent of freshmen have at least one card, but 56 percent of seniors carry *four or more*.

Undergraduates reported direct mail solicitation as the primary source for selecting a credit card vendor. The second most common source was their parents.

Only 21 percent of undergraduates with credit cards reported that they pay off all cards each month. Most said they make at least the minimum payment, but 11 percent reported paying less than the minimum required each month.

Students' estimates of their outstanding credit card balances in a survey were significantly lower than the average credit card balance as reported by their credit bureaus.

Source: www.nelliemae.com . A study by the Nellie Mae Company, 2005

---

parents can combat unrealistic economic expectations is by teaching realistic costs. Children should be made to bear the costs of their purchases, to some extent, from an early age.

As I discussed in my book *Family Rules*, we Americans have trouble putting limits on our children and saying "no" when they want something. "Get a baby-sitting job or mow lawns and use your earnings for that" sounds right to us in principle, but we hate to be guilty of delaying their gratification. So many parents lead their pre-teens to expect every new video game or toy that comes along, as a matter of entitlement. The kids know they may have to nag awhile, ignore a few "no"s and "we'll see"s, but eventually the parents will open their wallets.

Divorce has made this problem worse, if two parents don't coordinate their answers. Or if they compete to be the one who says Yes.

Nick: paying for the essentials

Don't blame us if your generation led us to expect a certain kind of lifestyle. Like a cable hookup, for example. A cable package with all the sports and movie channels would cost the same coming to my apartment as it does to Dad's house, close to $100 a month. It's a small item in his budget, but I can't afford it right now. If I grew up thinking all those channels (and a big screen to view them on) were among the basic necessities like food and shelter, I'm in trouble.

Ignorance. The second way our "buy now, pay later" economy feeds upon the young is by taking advantage of their ignorance. The rest of this chapter will deal with preventive education, but let me say here that the best way for parents to combat ignorance about financing is to point out the ubiquitous and aggressive promises of EZ-Credit, no interest payments or no payments at all for twelve months, and my favorite: "Bad Credit? No Problem!" Ask the young person why that loan office in the strip mall is so eager to make loans to people with bad credit histories.

For those in the business of exploiting consumers' innocence and vulnerability, the three best groups of people to take advantage of are the elderly, the young, and the broke. If your kid falls in two of those demographics, he or she is a doubly attractive target for overpriced goods and services, loans on bad terms, and phony money-making schemes.

Nick: *mano a mano*, versus GE

I was sleeping on a futon on a wooden slat frame that wasn't comfortable, and it wasn't even my futon, so I knew that I wanted to get a bed. I didn't necessarily plan on buying a bed right then, but I passed a bed store every day to and from the subway, and I went in there and started trying out different beds. I reached the conclusion that it was worth it to me to spend some major money on something that I would have for a long time; I wanted exactly the right bed for me to rest my body so that I could go out into the world and make more money.

I tried all the beds in the store and really liked this $1,599 mattress. I talked with the saleswoman briefly, but I knew I couldn't afford it right then. So then she started talking to me about payment plans. I started thinking about it, and I felt it was in fact worth $1,599, and over the course of two years I could totally afford it. As I understood her, "There's no rule about how fast you have to pay it off or how soon you're allowed to pay it off."

Ultimately, you give them your name and address and they copy your driver's license; she threw in a couple of pillows and a box spring, and I upgraded the frame and got a cover for the mattress. It came to about $1,750. They delivered it a couple days later and then about a week after that I got a letter from a company called GE Money Bank which actually had a plastic card with a number on it. I thought, "Oh, that's interesting that the store's payment plan borrows the money from GE Money Bank and now I'm dealing with them."

I probably could have read the fine print or whatever came with the card and it probably would have said something about a minimum payment, but what it really came down to was that I wanted it to be a certain way and I just thought it was that way. The required down payment was small, but I had thrown down $300. You know, "I can afford $300, I'll just take a nice big bite out of it right off the top." Which is actually a pretty good policy if you are in that situation. But it doesn't roll over, you know? You can take all the bite you want, it still doesn't cover your next minimum payment.

I could have split that $300 into a few pieces or whatever, and doled it out every month, but I didn't realize that.

The minimum payment was like $40 or $60. And in the first couple of months, due to a whole bunch of other things that were going on in my life, I went through a period of being extremely broke, so I was glad I'd got ahead of those payments. Or so I thought. Then I got paid $2,000 for a website I'd built and I had some money again. So I called them up and said I want to pay the whole thing off. There was no interest for the first year, but my thinking was, "I have the money now so I better pay this or I'll spend it on something else and then I won't have it when they do start charging 20 percent interest or whatever."

I thought I knew exactly how much I still owed them, it should have been $1,450. But the guy on the phone said "You owe us that plus $130." It turned out that I had missed the minimum payment, and it had just gone by quietly. A couple of times. So this wasn't interest, it was the fine. The penalty. No phone call to tell me, "Hey, you may want to pay this because if you don't we get to charge you a whole bunch of extra money." The penalty was as much as the monthly payment would have been—but extra. Like, "Gotcha!"

I was careful to be polite to this guy, Fernando, on the phone. Beyond polite. I've worked customer service, and I know the customer service guy has a lot of power. But they can only use it selectively or else their bosses will get pissed at them. So if you're the caller, you want to be one of the nice people, to slip casually past that line and be one of the very few people who they actually help. It's really a matter of being very honest and humble. Because they hear excuses all day long and it's their job to tell you to screw yourself.

Somehow he heard my story, which revolved around the fact that I did pay them off and I wasn't trying to make trouble. "Look, I was really trying to be a good borrower of money, you know? I paid it all back within four months, didn't stretch it out for the whole year of zero interest like I could have." And he was ultimately reasonable and agreed to close the account and waive the penalty. So I wound up free and clear without paying a dollar more than the original purchase price.

I didn't find out how they messed me up until many months later, when I applied for an American Express business card and they went through the process of checking my credit report. This isn't the type of card they mail to college kids trying to rope them in at 19.75 percent APR or whatever. They're more upstanding, so, being upstanding, they didn't let me into their club. Their website's report said "too many negative credit scores."

So I went through the process of contacting all three credit bureaus, which was interesting: all three seemed to agree. There was a bank account I'd had in Colorado with Wells Fargo, which is another story. Then there was a Comcast bill or something, and then there was GE Money Bank. The way it works is, every month is either a green or a red square. If you're good, you get a green square and if you're bad you get a red square and they rate you thirty or sixty or ninety or however many days late you were for that month. On my line for GE Money Bank, the months were like Good, Bad, Bad, Done: account closed, which looks terrible. What I ended up having to do was contact all three credit agencies (even though you can tell they're in some kind of cahoots) and submit this form to each of their web sites telling them their information was incorrect. And then I had to forward them a letter from GE Money Bank which indicates that I in fact am not a bad person. So I called GE Money Bank, "You guys did this and this and it's really messing me up, I don't want to bother you but could you please …" I had learned how to be a pain in the ass, while remaining calm and patient and polite. I sit down with some snacks and water and

I'm prepared to stay on the horn for hours. I'm so sweet, real nice, but I won't go away until they do what they can do. If you get abusive, then they get calm, because company policy allows them to hang up on you. But when you know you're not going to get anything accomplished fast, and you're willing to hang out with them for hours and be polite, they get frustrated. So I did that, and eventually somebody there corrected the problem.

Usury. The third way our borrower economy preys on our young is by feeding most aggressively on those who can least afford to borrow. The rich borrow at extremely low interest rates, thus staying rich by *using other people's money*—profitably. It's only the poor who pay double-digit rates. For example, they have to go to a storefront loan agency to get their cancelled phone service reconnected or to put food on the table. *Other people's money is using them* (to get more money out of them).

As I explained above, lending to those who can least afford to borrow is an enormously profitable business. Especially since lenders can count on parents to bail out those twenty-somethings when they get in trouble.

We are *right* to help them with lower interest loans (or even gifts, if we choose), especially in early adulthood or the first time it happens. But *how* we do so—the Deal—is central to the difference between real helping and mere enabling. We'll say more about parental loans in the next chapter.

Preventive education – starting early

Elementary school kids can learn the principles of prudent spending and financing, in a general way. They can understand all the relevant math and practical examples when they're in high school. Then they need mentoring when they go forth into the world with checkbooks, debit cards and bills to pay.

For readers who still have younger children, I'll briefly list the concepts parents need to communicate about money in the elementary years:

Cash flow. Young children see that some people have more money than others (notably, adults have vast quantities of it and children barely have any). But they tend to think of each family's money as a static supply like Fort Knox, that parents decide to dip into or not, for various purposes. An elementary school child is quite capable of learning that it's not a big pile of gold ingots somewhere, it's really about money flowing in and out, income and expenses. Take every opportunity to explain that. When they refer to how much your family "has" (which is, of course, always less than some people and more than many others), explain that it's a matter of matching income to needs, rather than how much we "have".

I'm not suggesting you give an economics lecture. But you can illustrate the concept of cash flow when the kid receives some money and spends part or all of it. Even more valuable, I think, is sharing some of the factors that enter into your own economic decisions—for example, when thinking of trading in your car.

Comparison shopping. This is just a matter of thinking aloud: mentioning what you're doing as you compare prices in stores or in catalogs. Thus they see you (their role model for how to be a grown-up) compare and analyze rather than buy impulsively.

Earning. By the time children begin to earn money for chores or neighborhood jobs, make sure they get the direct connection between that money and the *time* they worked. The neighbor who pays your twelve-year-old $20 for a half-hour's work cutting his grass, or pays day nanny rates to an eighth grader for sitting with a sleeping baby for a couple of hours, does them and you a disservice. Help the child set a rate or a price that reflects the market value of whatever they're selling.

Planning. As Joline Godfrey points out in her book *Raising Financially Fit Kids*[31], the pre-teen child is capable of grasping the

---

31   Ten Speed Press, 2003.

idea that families plan for changing needs years in advance. "I have to set aside money now for [*a tax bill in April* / *our vacation* / *whatever*]" or "Our income will be less in the winter because … ." or "Your sister starts college in four years; we're saving to pay for that, and then your college bills will start only two years later."

The cost of money. An elementary school child can understand the basic concept of interest: Whoever borrows money—a business owner, a homeowner, a customer of that storefront with the big LOAN$$ sign—pays back an amount more than he borrowed. Whoever lends money, including the child who deposits her baby-sitting earnings in a savings account, gets paid back more than she loaned. And it adds up, over time, either as increments to the debt or the earnings. Children get the math by the time they're in middle school.

Worth, and work. We need to listen for, and correct, the idea that one is measured by money or what money buys. A sense of obligation comes with good fortune. This isn't merely a value proclamation to lessen our guilt about all those who have so much less than we do. The work ethic (whether working to make money or to make the community better) contributes to one's assessment of one's value: self-esteem. As parents, our children's self-esteem is our secret agent, protecting them when we can't do so ourselves. You won't be in the room when your child chooses between prudent or destructive behavior, from adolescence on. Your only agent on the spot will be the self-esteem you implanted in his or her early years.

Nick: getting and spending

I'm fascinated by this phenomenon of kids talking about other kids' families. "Oh yeah, they definitely have money." A family or a person attains "have money" status by never appearing to lack money. Depending on the community, people who "have money" could be a couple with a combined income of $40,000 a year who own a boat, some nice clothes, and are thrifty about other things. Sure, "has money" could be a Hollywood mogul or a thriving business owner, but it could also be a guy who drives a hot car, wears designer suits, buys pricey vodka at nightclubs, and tomorrow the bank's going to repossess his Lamborghini and foreclose on both houses, while the I.R.S. indicts him and his net worth turns out to be negative tens of millions. But that's tomorrow. Today he "has money."

In other words, it's all appearances. A girl can "have money" by putting a $3,000 dress on a credit card. It's ridiculous. For every family that's genuinely wealthy, how many appear to be so but are dangerously in debt?

I know, of course, there's a lot of real, multi-generational wealth in our country. Most of Dad's clients are people who have money because they keep it reproducing faster than they spend it (through wise borrowing and even wiser lending), and have been doing so for decades. Time is their secret! For the rest of us, it's easy to "have money" on any given day. The challenge is beating the sands that are slipping through the hourglass. To sustain life, resources are consumed. We have to bring in more than we consume.

For three years, I dated a girl from a much wealthier family than my own. Her father's extraordinary business success had given her a life of luxury, and paid the rent on her Manhattan apartment. Far from spoiled, however, my girlfriend was practical and sensible.

On a trip with her to Key Biscayne, where she had grown up, I was completely drained, financially as well as emotionally, trying to keep up with her old friends who were well practiced at "having money"—whether truly rich or not. In retrospect, my girlfriend wanted only my gracious company, not the competitive spending fury, which was due to my own insecurities at the time.

A great high-school course

If you have a high school student, find out whether the school sponsors a program that is offered for free by the National Endowment for Financial Education (NEFE) in partnership with the Cooperative Extension System of the U.S. Department of Agriculture and the Credit Union National Association. I think the content is excellent. To learn about this free program, check out http:/hsfpp.nefe.org.

Deals. You make Deals with your pre-teen children all the time, usually informally. Write them down, as with family rules. Contractual obligations with a parent prepare the child for accountability in adulthood.

EXAMPLE: The first warm day of spring, Carl leaves his bike in the yard overnight. By morning, it has pedaled away. The money he'll earn doing weekly lawn work for a neighbor will be enough to pay Mom back in a few months for advancing the price of a new bike. She writes up this Deal, including his promise to lock the bike in the shed without fail: "If left out and lost, it will not be replaced." (Printed out and signed by Mom and Carl.)

There's an implicit lesson there, about accountability. But there's an unfortunate lesson about borrowing: why is she *advancing* the money, removing the incentive, leaving poor Carl in the position of slaving in the hot sun only to make the payments on his vehicle?

BETTER: Pick up a cheap used bike for Carl, and make him demonstrate his new reliability in locking it up. Let him save his earnings to buy the new bike.

BETTER STILL: Mom's not willing to pay the whole cost of the new bike, but she feels it's unrealistic to expect Carl to come up with the price from his own earnings. So the Deal she offers is a matching grant: when he's raised half the money needed, she'll kick in the other half. (Deal printed and signed.) Thus she achieves three goals: gets him the new bike sooner

141

than he could on his own, avoids depleting all his summer earnings, yet makes him feel he "earned" the whole bicycle.

It's better to make Deals that involve the kid receiving whatever subsidy you might offer, *after* completing their part of the bargain. We all do the opposite occasionally, advancing money to be paid back later; but be aware that each time you do that, you're reinforcing the "buy now, pay later" message.

Once your child is an adolescent, you have more opportunities to make Deals that teach the value of being both respected and trusted. You can help them analyze whether the plan they're committing to for paying you back is realistic. And then you help by holding them accountable for doing so.

Motivation and support in adolescence

Preventive education continues through the middle and high school years by reinforcing the above concepts, with some additions.

Self sufficiency and citizenship. I like the way Joline Godfrey expresses this goal: "develop the capacity for economic self sufficiency." They're far from self-sufficient, but their *capacity* grows with each project they undertake. When we help them succeed at such projects, and emphasize what they themselves did rather than how much we did for them, we contribute as much to their future self-sufficiency as to their self-esteem.

Non-material assets. Productive skills are an asset. A college degree is an asset, a professional degree even more so. Work history is an asset. A reputation for responsibility is an asset. I'm not suggesting you preach or lecture about any of that, even once. Just point the fact out when the learner doesn't seem to recognize it.

EXAMPLE: Melanie is working for minimum wage, full time for the summer, behind an ice cream counter. She alludes self-deprecatingly to how little she earns.

MISTAKE: "That's all you can expect; you don't have any marketable skills yet. "

BETTER: "It's not just the money. You're building your resumé."

Nick: my thinking at seventeen:

If I got Dad to front $1,000 for used deejay turntables and amps, it would pay for itself in five jobs, $200 a night. I knew without question that I had the skills, so I assumed I'd also have the opportunities, and the discipline to get those five jobs and collect the $1,000. But I was leaving out the costs of getting to jobs, buying records, and having some money to spend every day.

Looking back, I think Dad was more interested in persuading himself that this was going to teach me something about either the rewards of enterprising behavior or the disappointment of inadequate planning than I was. I didn't really care about making a profit. I was just using whatever justification would persuade him to advance the money for the gear.

Debts arise between siblings and friends at this age. Should you get involved? I think you should. For example, you can insist that your daughter pay what she owes her sister before her credit is good with you. In accountants' terms, you would treat her account payable as a liability on her balance sheet. But don't treat an account receivable as an asset: "I'll be able to pay you back after school on Monday, Mom, when Terry brings me the $30 he owes me." Healthy skepticism is wise in that case, and if (as often happens) the debt from Terry is never collected, you want the full weight of that lesson to fall on your kid. (As we did in Chapter VIII, going over your older youth's table of Debts.)

Explaining wise versus dumb borrowing to adolescents. This is the time to introduce the difference between borrowing for investment—a productive expenditure—and borrowing for

---

Real mortgage rates

It's easy to show how asset appreciation determines the wisdom of a debt decision. Just compare the U.S. home mortgage situation in 2005 and 2007.

In both years, mortgage rates were around 6 percent. In 2005, however, home values were appreciating at more than 16 percent. So the real mortgage rate was 6 *minus* 16; in other words, a *reversed* 10 percent. You got a 16 percent return on your investment (down payment) in the home, plus a 10 percent *profit* on the money you borrowed. (You only paid 6 percent for something that was increasing in value by 16 percent.) Who wouldn't want to buy real estate in that world?

In 2007, the home's market value *dropped* by almost 9 percent. So the financing decision produced a net *loss* of almost 15 percent that year (the drop in asset value combined with the cost of the loan). If one had only known!

---

consumption. I would state the difference between wise and dumb borrowing this way to a young person: borrowing is wise only if

- it's virtually certain that one can make the scheduled payments *and*

- the money borrowed is used for one of three purposes:
  - to increase one's earning power in the future; or
  - to provide for genuine needs, such as housing, that can only be met if financed in this way; or
  - to acquire assets that will appreciate in value, or at least won't depreciate much.

The dumbest borrowing is that which meets none of those purposes *and* saddles the borrower with more debt than he can service.

Your family economy offers an adolescent two sources for learning about debt. One is their borrowing from you and their friends: hold them accountable. The other source of information, more representative of adult life, is your own borrowing. Do you have a mortgage? Car loan? Business loan? Credit card debt? After explaining that your finances are no one's business outside the family, share this information with your teenager, confidentially (you needn't disclose the dollar amounts). Talk about your own current loans, as well as any mistakes you may have made in the past that you came to regret. It's more effective to convey the important principles when you're revealing your own sound or regretted economic behavior, than it will be if you wait to lecture the kid who's already over his head in debt.

The criteria listed above can be explained to a child of middle school years. By high school and college, they grasp it immediately—in principle—but still may need to see concrete examples.

> EXAMPLE: Sheldon disputes his son's need for a nicer snowboard. Chris wants his parents to advance three months' allowance. Sheldon says, "We don't go into *debt* for something that only provides enjoyment. We pay for that with money we previously saved. A workman takes on debt to pay for something that will increase his income, like tools or a truck. We might take out a bank loan for something that will save us money, like if the whole house needed new insulation, or when we went from renting to buying a house. Even then, we only borrow when we know where the money will come from that we'll use to pay off the loan. For anything else, we wait until we have the money saved up before we spend it."

By the time they're out of high school, your kids should understand the basics of any loan you currently have—not to scare them, but to show your reasoning about it.

Cost of money. Every dollar spent is a dollar that's not growing more dollars. Every dollar borrowed is borrowed at interest; and interest *compounds*. What will this loan actually cost you, as a rate? What will it amount to in total dollars? And how much are the payments in proportion to your total budget? In

Nick's example of borrowing $50 to buy a concert ticket, the interest rate of 2 percent per week exceeded that of all but a mob loan shark, yet it didn't matter at that level. Ensuring a seat at the concert only cost him an extra dollar. But in other instances, even a modest single digit annual interest could require payments that are beyond the youth's cash flow. A car would allow him to get to a better paying job across town, so it's arguably an investment, and the APR finance rate is only 7 percent—great, but if he can't afford the monthly payment on top of insurance and gas, buying the car will hurt more than help.

Depreciation. And what will happen to the value of the thing you're buying, over the time it takes you to pay for it? A house will probably gain value in the long term (though not by much, when maintenance and taxes, as well as inflation, are factored in). So a loan to buy or improve your home makes more sense than to buy something that depreciates quickly in value, as a new car does. And what if you're making payments on a car loan whose balance is greater than the depreciated value of the vehicle? (Can your kids explain what someone means who says "I'm upside down on my car loan"?)

A trip to Hawaii that takes $4,000 out of my savings account is relatively easy to evaluate, depending on the size of that account and my subjective enjoyment of the trip. But it's a different matter if I'm still going to be paying for it, with interest, two years later. Will those memories and snapshots be worth $200 a month then?

Credit cards. You almost certainly get credit card offers in the mail, though only a fraction of the number your kids will start to receive as soon as their names and addresses show up on lists of college applicants, new drivers, or checking account holders. Open some of those and read them aloud. Point out their fallacies, hidden costs, and risks.

The first time your child receives a credit card offer—and definitely before they go away to school—talk about what a scam it is for the company to solicit someone in their position. Prepare them to be as suspicious as when they were little and you warned them about never getting in a stranger's car. "No nice person asks a child to get in his car," you said. Now tell them that no nice business asks a youngster to go into debt. Truly, the law ought to deal harshly with lenders who prey on the young. Unfortunately, most of them operate within the letter of the law, but that only makes them more dangerous. The monkfish lies on the sea floor: huge, flat, and camouflaged, a stalk rising from the top of its head, waving a flag-like fin back and forth. It's a lure, drawing other hungry fish to come hither, where the monkfish opens its capacious mouth and snaps them up. It's a fish-eat-fish world out there, don't kid yourself.

Nick: parental warnings

Telling teenagers they're not old enough to have a credit card does about as much good as warning them off alcohol or sex: anything my parents tell me I'm not old enough to do must be good. So don't say "you're too young," say "you're too *intelligent* to be suckered by those misleading offers that come in the mail."

After high school: earning and spending

There are two ways, and only two, to stay out of debt: Earn more. Or spend less.

I don't mean to be flippant—neither of those solutions is easy to accomplish—but mentoring learners with their checking accounts and their debts puts the question at the forefront. As with Jill in Chapter VII, should this young person, at this particular point in her life, concentrate on earning more, or on spending less?

If she's a full-time student working part time, or a part-time student with a full-time job, it might slow her education if she pursues more lucrative employment right now. Assuming the student is enrolled in a program that will increase her earning power, she should probably look at ways to cut her expenses while staying in school.

Conversely, a young person who isn't in school, and who makes too little to support basic living expenses, might better look to the income side of the balance.

You, as mentor, have much to offer on both questions, drawing on your own experience, wisdom, and personal contacts. I've found, however, that it's easier to help with career advice (the earning side) than it is to mentor young people on the spending side.

> EXAMPLE: One of my young clients, having broken up with the boyfriend who had shared her rent, said she would have to look for a better paying job. Having been with her employer less than a year, she hadn't thought of asking for a raise. I pointed out that she'd been given more responsibilities, twice, since starting the job. "When they hired you, they didn't know if you'd be worth the $400 a week; you've shown them that you're worth that much and more. Since you like working there, give them a chance to keep you."
>
> She said she had thought of telling them she couldn't afford to stay, she needed to earn at least $80 a week more. "That's not the best approach," I explained. "Your rent isn't their problem. Tell them you believe you've shown what value you can bring to the office, and you'd like to stay and continue growing with their business, as long as you're compensated accordingly. It's about your value to the company, not about your own needs." (I don't think many young employees realize that.)

Nick: cutting down expenses

Buy durable stuff that will last for years (like bookcases) or cheap stuff that you plan to throw away as soon as you can afford to do so. Nice furniture will get banged up in frequent moves or won't stand up under abuse by roommates and party guests.

If you can only buy something on the installment plan, you're better off doing without it.

If you want something because it will make you feel less like a young person and more like a real person, but can't really afford it, remind yourself how being broke makes you feel.

Your collection (of music, clothes, ski equipment, shoes) is not you.

Consider the cost per use. A $200 snowboard may be a terrific deal, but not if you'll only get a chance to use it once this year.

Learn how to maintain clothing: stitches in time, stain removal, vinegar to take salt stains off leather, and so forth. Take care of what you have!

Buy groceries in bulk, and make most of your meals at home.

If you live in a city, take a cab whenever public transportation is inconvenient. If you never treat yourself to a taxi, you're likely to come to believe you need a car. I guarantee taxis don't come close to the cost of owning, driving, maintaining, and parking an automobile of your own.

No doubt, you also have sensible advice to impart about living frugally. But two problems arise in your relationship with a learner who has chronically spent more than he or she can afford. One problem is that advice about frugality falls on deaf ears. Sure, many young people are extremely frugal. But your kid isn't one of them. *Maybe* he or she will put some of these suggestions to good effect; on the other hand, frugality may run counter to powerful concerns about self image and cultural models.

The other problem is that you might not be the best spokesperson for frugality, because there's no sign of it in your own behavior. If you don't live the philosophy, you may not be able to preach it convincingly. On the other hand, if you live extremely modestly, to the point of doing without comforts that are more or less standard in your community, your kids may

---

Additional ways to cut costs

Consider depreciation. The best example is an automobile. A used car worth $5,000 on the lot is still a $5,000 asset after you buy it. A new automobile loses 10 percent to 20 percent of its value in the first mile you drive it. Both cars will lose another 15 percent to 20 percent of their resale value each year. Similar depreciation occurs with other major purchases, such as an entertainment system: the cost of like-new used components may be half that of brand new ones, and they won't lose any further value for many years.

Insurance policies: analyze them carefully based on your need, what kinds and amounts of coverage, what's the deductible, and so forth. For example, you probably don't need collision insurance if you've got an already banged-up car (see Chapter XI).

Nothing beats a full-time job with a full-fledged company. Self-employment has some advantages, but they disappear quickly if your disposable income doesn't support your medical expenses (insurance premiums and co-pay) or your interest payments on debts. Most employer health plans are superior to anything an individual can buy. And members of employee credit unions have access to loans, when necessary, at reasonable rates.

---

resent having grown up that way, which leads them to reject your ideas on the subject.

The truth is that I don't have suggestions for *teaching* them to stop spending money on things you regard as unnecessary vanities at this point in their lives. I'm thinking of the CD and DVD collections that represent several thousand dollars of excess spending over income. Or her wardrobe full of chic clothes, worn only once, or never worn. Or the trip to the Bahamas with roommates, charged on the already-loaded credit card. I agree with your thoughts about such expenditures. But can you raise them constructively without taking on that role of Censorious Parent to be Avoided?

A good psychological counselor would concentrate on listening, understanding, and empathizing with the young person's desires. Occasionally, she'd ask about the client's feelings: "Is it frustrating, wanting the trappings of a comfortable life but still stuck in the starving student phase?" "Would it be hard for you socially, to pass up a trip like that and confess that you just can't afford it?" "Do people judge you by what you wear? Do you judge yourself by what you wear?"

I'm not the best at non-prescriptive, empathic listening (which may be why I write books telling people how to behave sensibly). In this case, my prescriptive advice to you is not to give young people prescriptive advice about what they spend their money on—nor about whom they spend it with. Instead, focus on your Deal and follow through on your side of it. Focus on making the learner's economic reality as salient as you can through the numbers on those bank statements. Let them draw their own conclusions, while you concentrate on supporting their self-esteem and respecting their increasing trustworthiness.

When they ask for advice, of course, we do have many suggestions about cutting expenses (see box for my additions to those Nick made above). And you can also teach by setting an example; they've been watching you, from early childhood on.

Helping youth collect money owed to them

One of the biggest challenges Nick faced, when he was doing a variety of jobs for a variety of clients, was getting them to pay him before his own bills became overdue. On one occasion both his phone company and his Internet provider shut him off. He couldn't do the assignments he had, and no new prospects could reach him.

A young person often has no idea how to collect from someone who promised to pay for work, then takes their time doing so. It's so discouraging to be stiffed by such a person that the victim may go into denial, trusting that the exploiter will mail a check "if I don't hassle him too much." He'd like to believe that the man or woman is like any other trusted friend. This may be an education for you, the parent, as well, if you've never had to be

---

What's a good buy?

You see a great deal on a designer-label coat: half price! But the right question isn't about the difference between its advertised "retail" and "sale price," it's about the cost per wearing. A more versatile coat may be the better buy, even if it costs more. This may be obvious to you (I hope it's not a revelation), but I'll bet it's not how your kid has looked at clothing purchases.

Sam has three winter jackets, on which he "saved" a total of $500 by buying them on sale. Total expenditure: $700. Pat spent the same amount on two winter coats, better made, that will hold up over many more wearings. Who cares that they weren't "on sale"?

---

assertive about collecting a debt. (Nick talked about this problem of self-employment in Chapter VI.)

When Nick was in high school, he had two experiences with employers who kept dodging his attempts to collect the money they'd promised him for some manual labor. All it took was my telephoning, politely: "I understand Nick did _____ hours of work for you, at $____ an hour. Is that correct?" It's possible you may learn that the facts, from the other adult's point of view, don't match what your kid led you to believe. In my experience, they did; and on both occasions, the employer mumbled something about waiting for my son to come by for the money, or not knowing the address to send a check. I didn't need to do anything more than clarify the details. I had delivered the message, one adult to another, that it wasn't acceptable to take advantage of a kid's trusting nature.

By the time they're in college or out in the world, they'll make those calls themselves; your role as mentor is merely to assure them that it's appropriate and necessary. You might even role-play the conversation with them if they're reluctant to press for payment for freelance work, or their final check from an ex-employer they're not keen to talk to. Or a security deposit after they move out of an apartment. Persistence may be required.

If polite discourse doesn't work, your county courts can be effective. You might help your son write a letter to the delinquent payer, announcing his intention to file suit in small claims court if he doesn't receive a check by such-and-such date. There are fees for filing, and it takes time, but it can be worth doing if it's a matter of many hundreds of dollars. Filing a small claims suit can have psychological value for your son and your relationship with him, regardless of the monetary return. You're assuring him that

- he's entitled to be paid for his work.
- collecting receivables is part of what financially mature people do.
- you'll stand up for him if he has been treated unjustly.

MISTAKE: It's a bad idea to lecture about what the youth should have done. "You should have shown him his finished website, but not put it up on his server until he paid you. And you didn't get an agreement from him in writing. Now you'll never get paid." Regardless of the truth in that, it's blaming the victim. Your child doesn't need any more lectures about his many failures. This is a time to show your support, which, as I said in Chapter IV, is often better shown by giving time and counsel than by opening your own wallet.

Loans among friends. Unlike the problem of collecting from an employer, I wouldn't get involved when the debt is between your youth and a friend. I've mentioned that young adults, even when not yet as trustworthy as we'd like, want very much to be trusted and are often too trusting of others. They believe that their own word is sacred and they can count on their friends. Unfortunately, experience often contradicts both those beliefs.

Yes, they have the best of intentions regarding their own debts; therefore we should reinforce those intentions and never suggest that paying back their friend is of lower priority than the phone company, or ourselves. And yes, they assume the friend who owes them money will regard it as an equally high priority; therefore we

---

Teaching kids the power of compound interest

Just in case they weren't paying attention in math class, you should check to be sure your young adult knows what interest is, how it compounds, and the reason repaying a larger portion of the principal each month costs much less in the long run.

When the interest rate is low, compounding is a trivial technical matter. But when the annual rate gets up into the range typical of consumer loans, compounding makes a big difference. Just as compounding works in our favor when we have a long-term certificate of deposit or retirement annuity, where the interest stays in the account and builds interest on interest, it works against us when we have a debt that accrues interest on interest.

I teach the concept of compound interest this way: You borrow $100 for one year at 12 percent annual interest. How much interest do you owe after one month? Since there are twelve months in a year, the interest each month is one-twelfth of the annual interest: one percent, $1.00 on a $100 loan. Now, in a "no payments for twelve months" deal, how much is your loan balance after two months (even though you don't have to start making payments yet)? Two dollars? No: you've also accumulated a month's interest on that dollar you didn't pay last month.

---

don't express our doubts about that friend's trustworthiness, we merely say "We can't count on the timeliness of receiving that money, since you have no control over when he'll be able to pay you."

In other words, when Nick and I were going over his financial situation and he said a friend owed him money, I would not count that as a "receivable". However, when he owed money to one of his friends for any reason—was late in paying his share of rent, for example, or had "bought" the friend's couch or speakers but hadn't yet produced the money—we counted that as a serious debt, just as if it had been a legally enforceable contract.

Loan decisions

In Chapter VII, Nick explained how he determined his discretionary spending, the difference between his current income and his monthly obligations. Now in his mid-twenties and working constantly, he takes the "can I afford it" question one step further: "If I can't afford it, should I borrow to buy it?" As this table shows, he decides whether the expenditure in question is something with an economic benefit or just a desire. We both agree that if debt has a place in the lives of young adults, it's in regard to those needs that they hope will have economic benefits, not in regard to mere desires.

	Purchases that have economic benefits	Purchases that fulfill non-economic desires
If income is sufficient	***priority uses for cash*** • food • microwave, pots and pans • bicycle • birthday card for Dad	***do not charge; buy with left over cash*** • eating out • entertainment • new clothes
If income is not sufficient	***shop for affordable loan*** • education • condo • used car or truck • work tools	***postpone!*** • big vacation • wedding • prestige car • brand new furniture • expensive skis • latest fashion in clothing

He's saying that not only would he pay cash rather than charge things like restaurant meals, he'd also make sure the cash was really discretionary, left over after paying for necessities. The items listed in each box are merely examples, and what is affordable or of economic benefit to one person will be unaffordable or not an economic benefit to someone else. In which of those boxes would you put the purchase of a computer, for example? Does your daughter need a new, state-of-the-art laptop, or would a used desktop for a few hundred dollars be sufficient? Is it really needed for work or education, or merely for Facebook chats? If it's an educational expense (assuming this education will pay off in earning power), buying state-of-the-art might be wise; otherwise, perhaps she should settle for what her current income affords, or postpone it.

Let's analyze some borrowing that's common among young adults, from the point of view of when it's a good idea to take a loan.

> EXAMPLE: At twenty-five, Frank inherited $120,000. He used it to buy a condo, putting down more than 50 percent of the purchase price, with a $1,000 per month mortgage. He was already paying 9 percent APR on a car loan and 12 percent on debt he accumulated during his last year of college. The lender was satisfied with Frank's $60,000 base salary and his unblemished credit report. But now mortgage rates have dropped, and his bank is offering a home equity loan at 6.5 percent, with which he could pay off both his 9 percent and 13 percent loans. No increased risk, and a reduction in both monthly and total payments: wise? Or dumb?[32]

> EXAMPLE: Sara just started working as a paid intern at an investment bank. Looking sharp is an investment in her future. Her favorite store offers 20 percent off today's purchases if you sign up for their credit card. She puts $2,500 worth of extremely well-made, practical outfits on the card. She plans to wear them many times, assuming the job, or another one like it, works out. The monthly interest on those purchases at 18.5

---

32   Answer: Wise. And that borrowing in his senior-year also proved to have been wise, even at 12 percent, as it allowed Frank to finish school so he could enter the job market as a college graduate.

percent is only $40, with a minimum payment of $65. But the first time Sara misses a payment, they smack her with a $60 penalty. She had $2,500 in her 3 percent money market account, but didn't want to touch that savings. This is the reverse of Frank's situation: Sara paid a high rate to avoid using money that was only earning a low rate. Wise? Or dumb?[33]

EXAMPLE: Bill's former roommate, totally trustworthy and brilliant, is starting a dot-com business. He gives Bill the opportunity to invest $10,000. Is that a good investment? It may or may not be, for someone who already has $10,000 and can afford to lose it. But for Bill to borrow that money through any combination of credit cards, family loan, or an increase in his mortgage payment, would be dumb. (See the section on Investing, below.)

One might assume that borrowing to finance higher education is always an example of wise borrowing, but it's not that simple; we'll delve into the complex topic of student loans in the last section of this chapter.

And what about borrowing for medical expenses, which can come up unexpectedly and catastrophically, in our nation where almost a third of families have no health insurance at all and at least as many have high co-pays or deductibles? Here, the question of wise versus dumb doesn't apply; the fact that anyone should have to take on catastrophic debt to pay medical bills is a national tragedy. Yet more than half (56 percent in a 2001 survey) of the million Americans who file for bankruptcy every year list medical bills as their reason for filing.[34] (We'll discuss health insurance in Chapter XI.)

The biggest thing *not* to do is what so many authors—sounding like spokespersons for the credit card industry—recommend. They say young people should have experience in "establishing credit and making the minimum payments." Anyone who is not

---

33   Answer: Dumb.
34   Seventy-five percent of those did have health insurance.

going to be able to pay for their consumer purchases in full is *never* wise to take a loan to pay for them. The mortgage they'll one day have on their home, sure: They'll need somewhere to live, and it's an asset that normally appreciates in the long run. A car that one needs for daily transportation—an investment in one's earning capacity—yes. Work tools, a business suit, yes. But borrowing for a vacation, a big fat wedding, a stake to bring to the Las Vegas poker tables? Not smart, and frequently disastrous.

Store loans

How about store loans, for major furniture or appliance purchases? Here's how I educated Nick and his sisters about this: "Suppose you're buying a bedroom suite in a furniture store for, say, $5,000. Wouldn't the store prefer you pay for it now, in full? Why do they offer to sell it for no money down and no payments for a year? Is it because they can't sell it otherwise, at that price? Or are they some kind of nonprofit, benevolent furniture provider to the poor?"

Neither is the case. When you pay cash, they're only in the furniture business; their profit is the price you pay minus all their costs. When they defer your payments, they're in the furniture business *and the finance business*. In many cases, they give up their entire profit margin on the bedroom suite in order to make the sale and take the heftier profits in interest charges.

Unfortunately, those customers who have the lowest credit ratings (and can least afford these purchases) are the ones who'll pay the 15 percent, 20 percent, 25 percent or more in annual interest rates. We surely don't want our children taking on debt at those rates.

It amounts to real money when the loan amount is several thousand dollars. Even at only 12 percent interest, the $5,000 bedroom suite, no money down, no payments for one year, has already created an obligation of $5,640 by the time the customer starts making those payments. The youth thinks, "I don't have to start paying off the $5,000 until a year from now." Wrong. A year from now, you start paying off $5,640.[35]

I don't mean to suggest that owning a retail furniture or appliance store is a license to print money. They have rent, payroll, and other costs. My point is to disabuse young people of the notion that "no money down, no payments for __ months" is some kind of a great deal.

Saving and investing

It's surprising, to me, how many young people want to start investing in some way—day trading or speculating in real estate seem to be the leading fantasies—while they're in debt. Perhaps I shouldn't be surprised. What better way to climb out from under the stress of credit card debt, or student loan payments one can't meet, or living from one paycheck to the next, than simply to get rich as soon as possible? They're surrounded by advertisements and articles about successful young investors. And, I'm sorry to say, a number of authors of advice books and columns suggest that one should begin early by setting aside a portion of each paycheck in a savings or investment account.

What's wrong with the advice to start saving and investing as soon as their earnings exceed their expenses? Nothing, if the young person has no high-interest debt. Even if they're paying 6 percent on a car loan or accumulating 8 percent on a student loan with deferred obligations, *if* their income exceeds their monthly expenses, then investing cautiously may make sense. However, it never makes sense to invest money one cannot afford to lose. Especially while one's debt is mounting at double-digit interest rates. The higher the projected rate of return on an investment, the riskier it must be, and therefore the stupider it is for someone with serious debts to put his money there.

---

35   Why $5,640 instead of $5,600 ($5,000 plus 12 percent)? That's the beauty of monthly compounding.

Of course, if I can *lock* a higher rate of return than my cost of borrowing, that is wise borrowing (assuming my living expenses are already covered). But that's a rare situation. More commonly, a locked rate (a certificate of deposit, for example) is a conservative rate, almost sure to be below the borrowing rate. An investor who goes after a significantly higher rate of return must accept a moderate risk of losing all or part of his investment. We grown-ups understand why that makes sense. We need to explain it to our kids, because it's not obvious: if I have $1,000 I don't need, and I believe the odds are five out of six that an investment will double its value in five years and only one chance in six of losing it all, then my expected profit[36] in five years is $667. After paying a 15 percent capital gains tax, that works out to a 9.4 percent annual return. A pretty good investment, *unless* the one chance in six occurs, and the loss of $1,000 causes me to be evicted from my apartment or miss payments on my MasterCard and be hit with penalties and a higher interest rate. In that case, even a relatively conservative investment is like playing Russian Roulette with one bullet in a six-chamber revolver.

Actually, wealthy investors don't take such risks. They own, say, $50 million in commercial real estate, on which their mortgage payments are substantially less than the rents they take in. Those properties are diverse enough so their bank is confident that even if one or two properties lose money, the owners' total income will never be less than what they owe the bank. Furthermore, most of the properties' market values will increase over time. So the bank is happy to lend them a few million more with which to buy the next property. The chance of the investor losing his down payment on properties acquired with mostly lenders' money is small; in fact, using his other property as collateral, he may have borrowed 100 percent of the funds for the next purchase. If things go well, what is his rate of return on the investment? Practically infinite: he invested nothing. If they don't go well, he could lose real assets. But

---

36   Five sixths of $2,000 plus one sixth of $0 = $1,667: a profit of 66.7% on the original $1,000 investment.

as long as he doesn't try to grow too fast, he's in no danger of being evicted from his home or missing payments on his MasterCard.

That's how the rich get richer, basically: with Other People's Money. Yes, they are taking risks. But they can afford to do so. Your twenty-five-year-old, who is living from paycheck to paycheck, cannot.

In other words, we need to teach them to save first, *then* invest as much of their savings as they can afford to risk, having ascertained that the expected return is greater than inflation *and* greater than the highest rate of interest they're accumulating on any of their debts, and be sure that in the worst case scenario, the amount they might lose will be bearable.

Credit cards

"I'm not saying teenagers getting credit cards is a bad trend," says one financial columnist and book author. "I think that kids should be learning young how to handle credit." She and just about every other author seem either to have been hoodwinked or co-opted by the credit card industry. I completely disagree: it is a bad trend. There is simply no way that putting purchases you can't immediately afford on a credit card should be called "learning how to handle credit." It's learning to be the *victim* of credit!

Almost every young person I've talked to, by his or her early twenties, has heard "it's important to establish credit" or "you need to have a good credit score." Those are distortions perpetrated by the lending industry, and by merchants eager to sell young people stuff they can't yet afford. Yes, it's important not to have a *bad* credit score; but *you don't need any credit score at all* until you shop for your first mortgage, if then. You might have to dance an extra step or two to get a lease on an apartment: show six months' paid utility bills, for example; or get your parent to co-sign your first lease, and use copies of the rent checks you write there to prove your reliability to the next landlord. But you don't need a history of credit card payments—that's a lie.

The big picture on investing

Here's an essential lesson I hope all my children will remember, if the day comes when they've saved enough money to invest:

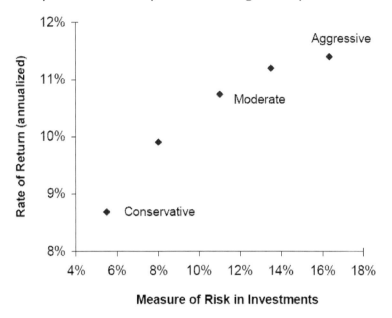

It's data from several million investors' experience over something like fifty years. Conservative investors keep half their assets in fixed-income stuff like bonds and annuities, and also keep a lot of cash in savings or money market accounts. Over the years, they average only about 8.5 percent a year in return. But it's fairly steady; they almost never have a losing year. At the other end are the aggressive investors who leave almost all their money in the stock market. Over time, they have a much better return (11.5% per year on the average). But they have to be willing to ride through some heavy loss years along the way.

—Data from Charles Schwab & Co., 2008.

Furthermore, *the only prudent use of your credit card doesn't produce a credit score*. The prudent use is as a way of conveniently charging expenses one will pay for in full by the due date each month.

If you're that responsible, one would think it would give you a stellar credit score, but on the contrary: by not carrying a balance forward, you're not considered to have had any credit.

I have just one card, which I use several times a day. It's worth the annual fee for its convenience alone, but it also gives me airline miles. I use it in the only way that makes economic sense: by paying the bill in full, before the due date, every month. Believe it or not, thirty years of such good behavior have left no trace on my credit rating, either way. I get no "credit" (in terms of a rating) for paying my bills in full, because I didn't take on any debt! Yet I'm actually borrowing thousands every month, interest free for two to five weeks, because no interest is charged until my monthly due date. However, if you carry a balance (even if you religiously make those minimum payments) they start charging interest *on every charge, beginning on the day a merchant posts it to the account.* Did you know that? Nobody tells young people these details.

Sure, you're building your credit score; but at what cost? Especially considering the fact that as soon as you have a problem making a payment, you get a black mark that sits on your credit report for seven and a half years, doing infinitely more damage than any benefit you got by "establishing credit."

What are secured versus unsecured loans?

We need to explain to our youth why they have to pay 18 percent interest or more when they charge store purchases or restaurant meals, but less than half that rate on a $10,000 car loan. It's because the latter, like a mortgage, is *secured* by the value of the asset, called *collateral*. As a borrower, one tends to prefer an unsecured loan rather than having an asset at risk of being repossessed, as is the case with a car loan. But *an unsecured loan costs much more.* The charges on credit cards are *unsecured*—the food's been eaten, the flight's been flown—so the company has to cover its risk by charging higher interest.

At least, that's the theory. In actuality, credit card companies cover their risk several times over: by a surcharge between 1 percent and 2 percent to the merchant, by penalties (far in excess of the cost of money) for late payment, by selling their delinquent accounts to collection agencies, by lobbying Congress to make bankruptcy laws more restrictive, and by investing in a scary credit reporting system that punishes the guilty (and frequently sullies the innocent by mistake).

The bottom line is that credit cards are the most profitable line of business for banks. That's why we all get the stream of invitations to activate new credit cards. It's interesting that the one thing those "preapproval" letters don't tout, and often don't mention, is the interest rate. In contrast, auto companies, appliance stores, and mortgage ads lead with the numbers—their competitive current rate and low down payment or interest deferment—and the limitations follow in fine print. The credit card inducements are just the opposite: airline miles and other benefits for frequent users, customized pictures on the card, donating a tiny fraction of your payments to a worthy cause, or discounts on certain purchases. The interest rates are so outrageous that you have to search through the fine print to find them.[37]

Practically every major retailer and gas station chain now urges us to sign up for their labeled credit card in addition to whatever other cards we carry. They suggest it's worth taking theirs even if we only plan to use it in their store or on their website. But, think about this (I say, as I educate young people about credit cards): would they offer $50 in free goods, or steep discounts when we use the card to shop there, if their motive were only to get our business? Surely they'd rather receive full price, in cash, than a discounted price a month later. The explanation is that the issuer counts on most people (a) to use that card elsewhere as well,

---

37   When you do, you'll find it isn't a guaranteed rate—they'll set your rate after you agree to activate that "pre-approved" card. And they can change it later. You're the one being asked to pre-approve the deal.

when maxed out on other cards, and (b) to carry a balance on the card, so they become high-interest borrowers.[38]

Nick: first credit card

I had a checking account with Wells Fargo. They offered me a card with a $1,000 limit, so I thought about going to California to visit a friend. I figured I'd buy a round-trip ticket and then when I got there I'd use the card up until I hit the limit. Because when I got back to Boulder there were going to be a couple of paychecks waiting for me and I could pay it off. It wasn't a good deal, it was a terrible interest rate. So I went to California, used the card until it was denied, and as soon as I got back I paid it off. What I screwed up was, I didn't cancel it. I didn't go over all the details with them, you know what I mean? Just kind of took the rest of it for granted, like they knew what I was thinking or something. After all, I had done the main important thing, which was pay it off. I guess for a credit card with a zero balance, you don't receive anything in the mail. If you don't use it, they're still hoping you'll have to. If I got any letters from them up to the time I moved out of state, I probably didn't bother to open it since the account was history as far as I was concerned. I know after I moved I didn't get any letters from them. But three years later, when I applied for an American Express business card, my credit report showed Wells Fargo: Paid, then thirty-six months of empty squares, and then a violation. Because they just busted me, apparently, for not telling them I wasn't going to use it any more. It wasn't even a monetary fine. I called them, and I didn't owe them any money, there wasn't a collection

---

38   Wal-Mart and other companies don't merely send a credit card, they mail a few preprinted checks with your monthly statement, encouraging you to "simply write a check on the account any time you need to transfer balances from other credit cards or make a large purchase." They ought to be prosecuted for racketeering.

agency out after me or anything, they just put a
black mark against me for not canceling the card
in the proper manner. I still have that card, in
the archive of my life.

I'm not preaching "never finance anything, always pay in
full or do without." Most people don't have that luxury in their
personal lives. I'm preaching that *running an unpaid balance of any
amount on a credit card is not wise financing.* Period. If we do it in an
emergency, we had better know how we're going to resolve the
balance in a month or two, either through income that's in the
pipeline or by arranging more reasonable financing.

The myth about credit scores being a ticket to adulthood is
encouraged by the same folks who send "pre-approved" credit
cards to college students and even high school students. (Anyone
who hasn't defaulted recently is "approved".) We need to explain
to our kids, before they're out of their early teens, that those
lenders *want you in debt,* for one reason: the worse your debt, the
higher interest rate they get away with charging. They know a
small number of those "approved" borrowers will default on
their loans, but they've done the math: they can write off that
percentage and still make enormous returns on the penalties and
double-digit interest rates of those who don't default but only fall
farther and farther behind.

Furthermore, as I've said, with young debtors they know that
most of them have parents who will bail them out—as I'm going
to encourage you to do, in the next chapter.

Along with the myth of the "important" credit score is the
myth that as long as you're making your "minimum payment,"
you're "building credit." In reality, if you're only making the
minimum payment, you're avoiding a penalty but you're building
debt at a dangerous pace: interest upon interest upon interest.

Only you can explain this to your kids, early and often: that no
one, of any age, is smart to run a balance on a credit card. It's fine
to use the card for charges they can afford to pay in full, every

---

Handy calculator

www.bankrate.com has a calculator you can use to show your learner how long it takes to pay off a debt using minimum payment, and how much interest they'll have paid. For example, $1,000 on an 18 percent card with $25 minimum payment takes twelve years and $1,115 in interest. In other words, the purchase cost $2,115, more than twice the number on the price tag.

---

month, without fail. But for anything they really need and can't immediately pay for, there are more affordable ways to finance the purchase than by charging it on a bank card. If not, then the answer is "you can't afford it" rather than "you can charge it."

Nick: stick to cash

Dad argues against credit cards because of the high interest rate, the penalties, compound interest and all that. He has no problem charging purchases himself, because he knows he'll have enough money to pay for them when the bill comes. But someone in my marginal financial position is dipping into funds which I can't know for sure will be there. Sticking to cash and a debit card guarantees I won't make that mistake. If I blow my whole cash limit on music or a shirt, I'll have to subsist on the stale Cheerios in my cupboard for a couple of days, but at least I won't be spending myself into long-term debt.

Just say no

Even if credit cards haven't been a problem before, it might be a good idea to include "no credit card" as a condition in any Deal you have occasion to make with a young person who you think might be desperate or foolish enough to succumb to the temptation.

Too controlling, you ask? Remember what we're doing here: availing ourselves of the youth's need for our help, to exert leverage which will save both generations a great deal of grief.

There are places for letting children learn from their own mistakes, but running into the street when they were two years old wasn't one of them (it was the one exception to my "no spanking" rule in *Family Rules*), nor is running up credit card debt when they're twenty.

Other sources for consumer credit

A piece of advice for those who have good reason to make major purchases they can't immediately afford—for furniture, or a truck, or a computer, for example, or for medical bills—is to work where employees have a credit union. Credit unions offer reasonable interest rates to members, and you can make your payments through payroll deductions so you won't spend the money elsewhere and fall behind. This is a nice example to illustrate to learners that loan interest is inversely proportional to the risk. Any time you authorize direct deposit of loan obligations from your paycheck, that's a form of secured loan. Hence you can expect a lower interest rate.

Fortunately, your kids, if they enjoy your trust and seek your help with the challenge of making ends meet, may have access to the best financing bargain of all: the loan from a family member (next chapter).

Car loans

It's likely that at some point in early adulthood, an occasion for possibly wise borrowing might be for wheels. Following the decision matrix Nick presented earlier in this chapter, it makes sense to take a loan if one *needs* transportation, and can't afford the cash to purchase something safe and reliable. Of course, you need to forecast the monthly payments for the loan on top of fuel, maintenance, registration, insurance, and parking. Will all those costs be within the youth's means? It would be a tough setback for him to see his car or truck hauled away by the repo man.

The vehicle purchase decision, with or without a loan, is one for which good online help is available. The Internet offers numerous tools to help estimate depreciation, maintenance, and insurance costs for particular makes, models and years, state by state. Buyers can obtain that information before buying the car and signing the loan contract. (www.EarnTrust.net puts those numbers together to project their effect on the learner's bank balance over the months ahead; see Appendix.)

Student loans

One might assume that borrowing for higher education or technical training falls under the "wise borrowing" category, since costs are so high and the education, presumably, will increase one's earning power. But that's not necessarily true. It depends on the job market in one's field, and how much a degree in that field affects salaries. Can one make an economic argument, for example, for going into debt to get a four-year degree in acting from an expensive private college? Probably not, if one plans to use the degree for a career on the stage or in films. On the other hand, for a future high school drama teacher, the college loans may be wise debt.

It's tempting, when sending 18-year-olds off to the exhilarating but scary world of college, to shelter them from the financial decisions involved. But is it fair to encumber them with long-term obligations they don't fully comprehend, and might be reluctant to take on if they did? I believe that whether your college students will eventually be on the hook, or you yourself intend to be, it's critically important to make them full partners in the decision about student loans.

Student loans amount to humongous debt

In the United States, more people declare bankruptcy every year than graduate from college.[39] Sadly, some are bankrupt *because* they went to college.

Most families can't pay the full costs of college education, especially when they have two or more kids in college. They depend on an aid package of some kind, which probably includes a loan. Some 44 percent of all college students take out formal student loans, and an additional 20 to 25 percent incur other debt, including credit card debt, to get through school.

Due to the wealth gap in our society, five of every six African-American students and two out of three Hispanic students graduate with debt.

The average student borrower owes $27,600 on leaving college – more than triple what the amount was in the 1990s. The number who owe more than $40,000 has increased tenfold.[40]

The American Medical Association reported that the average medical student had more than $90,000 in student loans. One in seven owed more than $150,000. A student who borrows the whole amount needed for just the four years of medical school will be forty-three years old before she starts making a profit on the investment (if she's still practicing medicine).

Richard A. Davies, director of retirement and college savings plans for AllianceBernstein Investments reported, "Large amounts of college debt put graduates in a hole that can take years, even decades, from which to emerge." College costs are climbing much faster than the rate of inflation. One third of indebted college graduates say they've sold possessions to make ends meet; almost half say they're living paycheck to paycheck.

Because student loans are more consequential as well as more complicated than auto loans, it's extremely important that both

---

39   Report of the 2001 Consumer Bankruptcy Project, Harvard and New York University Law Schools and the Ford Foundation.

40   Source of the above statistics on college loan debt: www.nelliemae. com . A study by Nellie Mae, published May 2007.

parents and students educate yourselves about the alternative options, and their long term consequences.

What factors should you weigh before choosing? There are so many different kinds of loans, lenders, collectors, and repayment options that you need at least a whole book on those subjects.[41,42] In Chapter X, I discuss the problem of delinquency or default on student loan payments, and recommend some books and Internet resources on that subject. Here I only want to mention a couple of important things parents and students should discuss before taking on the loan:

Whose debt will this be: yours, your child's, or shared?

First of all, what's the Deal going to be, between student and parent? Will you be responsible for repaying those college, vocational, or graduate school loans? Or are you only helping your son or daughter research and obtain the loan, which he or she will have to repay? Perhaps the answer is that you'll split the payments in some proportion, even if the student is nominally liable for them. Or perhaps you want to make your contribution contingent on performance: "We'll repay that amount of debt which results in a degree (for example, the tuition loans for eight college semesters, if you graduate); you're responsible for all the debt if you don't finish, and for anything beyond eight semesters that you wind up requiring."

What you're willing and able to do for the student depends on your current financial situation, the number of kids you have, your own retirement security, as well as your child's track record in school and what kind of incentive you feel is needed, if any.

My advice, as always, is to *make this Deal explicit, in advance.* Of course, you can revisit the Deal year by year, based on how

---

41   A good book on shopping for student loans is *Paying for College without Going Broke* by Kal Chany. Princeton Review, 2005. You might also check out Athletic Scholarships for Dummies (despite the unfortunate title).

42   Murray Baker, *The Debt-Free Graduate: How to Survive College Without Going Broke.* The Career Press, 2000.

things go. (Equally true when you're paying for their education without a loan.) If your student's performance gives cause to doubt whether the money is well spent, the Deal for the second year doesn't have to be the same as it was for the first year.

It ain't the rates.

Understand, and be sure your student does, what the advantage of a student loan is. The rates aren't an especially good deal. The main benefit comes in the fact that students can defer making any payments on college loans until their entire higher education is complete, and longer if they enter certain postgraduate careers. But deferral means paying *more* eventually, not less. If the parents themselves plan to be responsible for the loans, borrowing against their home equity may be a better financial deal. The interest rate would be at least as good, the interest is tax deductible, and if your net worth is substantial, you're moving money out of your estate free of gift tax.

Aren't student loans basically a good deal? Yes, if both student and parent understand what they're undertaking. Obtained from the government, or a private lender affiliated with the school, the rates won't be as high as, say, credit card interest rates (the absolute *worst* way to finance expenses while in school), but they're no better than most collateralized loans, such as mortgages or car loans. In fact, one can think of that expected income gain due to the higher education as being the lender's "collateral" for these loans, because the law allows them to grab your tax refunds, garnish your salary, and prevent your re-enrollment for further education.

In other words, these loans are secured. The lender's risk is thus lower for student loans than for credit cards, so the interest rates are fairly reasonable. But they're no great bargain.

They offer three significant advantages over other types of loan:

- the obligation to repay them is deferred, at least until the student is out of school, and sometimes a year or two beyond that;

- within certain income and cap restrictions, the interest you'll pay will be tax deductible;

- if you enter certain public interest fields (health care, inner-city teaching, law enforcement), you can get longer deferments, interest reductions, and sometimes even total forgiveness of the loan. In many cases, the student doesn't have to have applied in advance and prepared specifically for that field (as would be the case, for example, with an ROTC scholarship), but can decide later to enter public service, in the face of the looming loan obligation.

Is private college worth it?

Even if your kids are so fortunate as to have you bear all the expense of their college, include them in the discussion about relative costs of different schools. Although they won't need financial aid, there's still the "opportunity cost" of money: what else it might have done for your family. For example, suppose you live in Illinois and your daughter is lucky enough to be accepted at both the University of Illinois and the University of Wisconsin. Both are large, state-run, socially similar campuses with the full range of academic and extracurricular opportunities. The difference in outlay over four years for an Illinois resident is $80,000. Investing that difference ($10,000 each semester) in a conservative 6 percent certificate of deposit would yield $91,591 after four years.

> MISTAKE: Princess is a good enough student to get letters of acceptance from both her own state's first-rate university and an equally first-rate university in another state. She's disqualified on financial grounds for a scholarship at either school. Princess and her friends think it's cooler to "go out of state." Mom and Dad can afford the $20,000 per year difference, and they don't want Princess to feel they're controlling her choice in the

matter. So they assure her, "we won't skimp on your higher education." They're cheating her of a valuable opportunity for financial education.

BETTER: Mom and Dad still give heavy weight to their daughter's preference, but they make sure she knows that the state university would save the family more than $90,000 over four years. Let's assume they are affluent enough that this isn't absolutely necessary. (Less affluent parents would explain that they *need* to take advantage of what their taxes provide in their own state.) Perhaps they tell their daughter this amount would be hers to spend on graduate school, or to invest in some other way. If they have younger children coming after her, they might give Princess only a portion of the savings, as they'll apply much of it to college education for the others. The point is to inform and involve their daughter fully in the economics of the decision.

I believe parents should disclose what the actual costs of college—tuition and everything else—are going to be, not merely as numbers ($50,000 or $100,000 or $200,000 of family money, per child) but relative to the family's resources, and relative to the economic value of the education.

MISTAKE: "Do you realize how much four years at Oberlin are going to cost? Almost $200,000!" The number in itself has no meaning.

BETTER: Is that a huge sacrifice for this family to make, or is it already available and planned for? Is she putting your financial security at risk, or are you merely trying to say she should study assiduously to get your money's worth? Express the number in terms of its impact on the student's future, and your own.

Cost of the debt

If the excess cost of one school over another would not be worth paying if you had the money, it's probably even less worth *borrowing* to cover it. Of course, there are other factors, but I can't think of a reason not to include a discussion of the economic value of the particular training and degree from a particular institution, among other factors in choosing a school and a means of bearing its cost.

If either of you is taking out a loan to cover much of the costs, that makes it even a *bigger* investment, not a smaller one. I'll bet your student doesn't realize that. Her thinking may well be, "it's only going to cost my parents $X a year; the rest will be covered by my financial aid." A loan is so-called aid, but in the form of debt! As with any debt, the question is whether what it enables you to buy will return value: either in greater eventual earning power, or at least in intangibles that will make the extra effort of repaying it worthwhile.

A rule of thumb these days is that a worker with a bachelor's degree will earn about 70 percent more, over his or her working life, than someone with only a high school degree. But the variation, across different careers and initial socioeconomic status, makes that average figure almost meaningless. What may be more useful is to consider, in advance, the monthly cost of repaying whatever money you have to borrow to get that degree, or the subsequent graduate degree. A rough answer to that question is about $125 a month per $10,000 borrowed, over a ten year period beginning about five years after you borrow it.

EXAMPLE: Terry takes federal student loans totaling $50,000 over the course of her four undergraduate years. She can expect to part with $625 per month out of her post-college earnings, for ten years; that's $75,000. (The consequences of delinquency or default are severe and relentless, as I'll explain in Chapter X.)

Terry defers payment on that undergraduate loan by going to law school. She plans to borrow $60,000 for her three years of law school. She reasons that if she lands the position with Megabux & Power's law firm, the extra $750 per month she'll pay (on top of the $625) will be chickenfeed, compared to the huge salary she's sure to make once she's promoted to partner. But when she quits law school after two years—having discovered that it's not the career for her, after all—the loan suddenly looms as a major problem.

A student–parent joint decision

Student loans are good deals for some, potential pitfalls for others. That's why I think it's a mistake for *either* the student alone or the parents alone to weigh the options. They need your participation and guidance; you need the assurance that they're entering into the contract fully informed. Remember that private student loan programs and private processors of federal loans, like all private lenders, are competing for profits. In 2007, U.S. Senate investigators reported widespread gifts and payoffs from some of those companies to college administrators, to steer families to them.[43]

When you go looking for a student loan, go directly to the Federal Department. of Education and whatever agency in your state may have an applicable program. If your college's financial aid officer attempts to steer you to a higher rate from a private lender, it's reasonable to question that person's competence, if not their integrity.

The bottom line

The age-old wisdom *caveat emptor* means "purchaser beware." A borrower is purchasing the use of money, with as much reason to be wary of risks and hidden costs as the proverbial buyer of a pig in a poke.

Education beginning in elementary school is the best preventive medicine for our nation's epidemic of potentially catastrophic debt. Concepts that everyone should be taught before adulthood include cash flow, comparison shopping, saving, planning, compound interest, inflation, and depreciation.

---

43 "Report Details Deals in Student Loan Industry." *The New York Times*, June 15, 2007.

The most important concept is the difference between wise and dumb borrowing. The definition of wise borrowing is *not*, as so many putative experts say, "establish good credit by making your payments reliably." It's "don't take on debt in the first place, if you might not be able to make the payments." Even if you can afford the terms of a loan, borrow only for purposes that will either increase your earning capacity (a required degree, training, tools, a truck) or build your equity in an appreciating asset. The best example of the latter is a home[44]: so long as the mortgage terms are reasonable, it's a conservative investment that's likely to appreciate modestly relative to inflation, while providing shelter at the same time.

Caution about the nature and extent of one's debts used to be part of our culture. Financing a home or business was normal, but living on credit was less acceptable than it seems to be today. If we could restore that attitude to American culture, it would reduce the profits of suburban shopping malls—and the credit card industry—but would go a long way to reverse our economy's precipitous slide relative to the rest of the world.

Realistically, of course, the culture is something you and I can't control. We can do a better job, however, of teaching our youngsters good judgment about debt.

Now, how do we help those who are already in trouble?

---

44   The great home mortgage bubble of 2000 to 2007 was the only exception in the past 100 years, due mainly to lenders driving home prices to artificially high levels, by duping low-income borrowers into low-equity loans at terms they would not be able to maintain.

X. Too Late for Prevention; What's the Treatment?

> *"My daughter is months behind in her bills, missing payments on her credit cards, and threatened with eviction. Is it a bad idea for me to bail her out? Is that what they mean by 'enabling'?"*
>
> *It depends what you think the problem is. One way or another, you'll help her to the extent you can afford, as well as coaching or finding someone to coach her through this crisis. But—what's your Deal?*

The previous chapter discussed ways to educate your kids, and work with them when times get tight, to prevent their winding up in the kind of debt that will really hold them back.

Unfortunately, it's too late for that advice. Your beloved fabulous kid is already ass deep in debt, or worse. What can you do? In some situations, the best thing you can do is pay the worst of his debts, or all of them, and let him pay you back, at a lower and slower rate than what his creditors require.

Different kinds of debt and degrees of debt demand different kinds of intervention. But let's begin with the general question: Is it wise to bail our adult children out of trouble they got themselves into? Or should one let them bear the consequences, so they learn?

Assuming this isn't a chronic problem, grab your bailing bucket. Absolutely. The lessons taught by overwhelming debt ("You paid too little attention to the income side of the equation and too little control to the expense side!") aren't taught any better by letting a bad crisis become hopeless. Debt isn't like water standing three feet deep in a basement, which has ruined the books and games stored there but will eventually flow away again and leave the owner with some cleaning up to do. It's a rising flood, threatening to carry off the whole house—literally. Left alone, it doesn't go away, it just gets deeper.

So, if your own financial resources are ample enough, of course you're going to help your child onto dry land. The question is, what kind of help? What's the Deal?

First of all, will you help with a gift (unconditional), a grant (a conditional gift) or a loan? Which of those is more constructive depends on your assessment of the circumstances.

Will these funds buy them out of trouble they should have known better than to have gotten into? In other words, are you reducing or deferring the consequences of irresponsible behavior? If so, a *loan* might be more helpful in the long run, as it prevents catastrophe while still leaving the ultimate responsibility with your child or their partner. (A half-gift, half-loan might be another such solution.) But if the disaster could not have been foreseen—there's no lesson that needs to be learned—obviously a gift is the most generous way to help.

If an addiction of any kind was involved in creating the problem, then the first question is whether it's now being treated. If the addict is rejecting treatment, I would not make a gift *or* a loan, because either form is likely to support nothing but the addiction. But if it is being treated, then a loan makes more sense than gifts or grants, to avoid inducing denial about what got the person in trouble.

> EXAMPLE: Ralph knows that clearing up an addict's debt, without facing the addiction head on, will only enable both the addiction and the debt to grow. When his son-in-law enters treatment, Ralph pays for the treatment itself, no strings attached. But he offers his daughter and son-in-law a low-interest loan, rather than a gift, to replace their mounting high-interest debts.

Another situation is where your youth needs money for proposed expenditures you're less than thrilled about. You don't think they are necessary or wise at this point. A loan might be better for your relationship than a gift would be. Major gifts are for anything parents want their kids to have at this point in life, without waiting until they can afford it.

> EXAMPLE: Susan can't make the payments on a new SUV her father thinks she had no business buying in the first place. He will ease the burden of that GMAC loan with a lower monthly payment DOD (Dear Old Dad) loan. But he refuses to enable her delusions of affluence by turning the car into a gift.

Finally, only call it a loan if both parties sincerely expect the money to be repaid. If your youth is unlikely to pay you back, believing you don't really expect it or will forgive and forget the debt if enough time goes by, then you'd both be better off calling it a gift or grant in the first place.

Gift versus grant examples

A true *gift* isn't supposed to have strings attached. A *grant* comes with certain conditions, as part of a Deal. So if we're talking about a gift that might have some accompanying conditions or limits, let's call it a grant. If no Deal is called for, it's a gift.

> EXAMPLE (unemployment help: *gift*): Julia and her husband are a hard-working, disciplined young couple. One of them loses a job when the local plant closes, shortly after they bought their first home. Her parents say, "If you would allow us, we'd like to make your mortgage payments until you've got two incomes again." Their son-in-law thanks them for the offer, but protests, "I don't know when we'd be able to pay you back." "You won't," they say. "This is a family thing."

> EXAMPLE (unemployment help: *grant*): The same situation, except Julia's husband would be more employable if he'd finish his degree before rushing back into full-time employment. Knowing he wishes he could afford to keep going for the degree, her parents offer to make the couple's mortgage payments as long as he works part time and takes the needed courses. He says he doesn't know when he and Julia will be in

a position to repay you. They say, "Our reward will be seeing you get your degree."

EXAMPLE (grant to a son in college): "We don't want you to lose the apartment *or* to drop out of school because you have to work more shifts. We will pay the back rent you owe, *if* you cut up your credit card, promise to pay rent before spending your paychecks on anything else, and put your academics first again."

EXAMPLE (health insurance gift): Kent mentions that he's missed his health insurance payment, among other problems. Unpaid premiums aren't debt; the policy will simply lapse immediately if his parents don't step in. Fortunately, their doing so is unlikely to be "enabling" in anything but a good way. Insurance is something the parents want to pay for, to minimize the financial risk of a catastrophic illness befalling their son. In the same way, they might provide the co-pay for a medical visit, if that's a hardship for Kent right now—without treating it as a loan.

What about the tax implications of our gifts? Consult your lawyer if the gift amounts to thousands of dollars, but don't let your decision about how much to give a child be dictated by tax implications. Nor should you diminish the kindness of your gifts by saying you did them for estate planning reasons, or to equalize the gift you made to another child. Each kid's situation at any particular time is its own case.

Loan examples

Compare these situations with the ones above:

MISTAKE (two poor decisions): Marty and his wife bought a $3,000 bedroom suite as their first anniversary present to themselves, then couldn't pay their regular bills for several months. Their electricity is about to be shut off. His parents write him a check for enough to cover three months' utilities. They say, "Consider this your anniversary present from us."

I would call that "present" *enabling*. The young couple's poor decision led the parents to make an equally bad one.

BETTER: Marty's parents offer a loan, sufficient to keep the repo men's paws off the furniture. They charge him a few percent of interest, so he won't forget the time cost of money.

EXAMPLE: Alicia wants a new laptop. Hers is slow, she says. Maybe so, but how much computing speed does a poet need? "We're not buying you another computer," her parents say. "If you really gotta, gotta have it, we do have sufficient funds to make you a loan at 3 percent interest. You surely can afford $20 a week. At that rate, it will take you ten years; you can pay us back faster when you get a better day job."

EXAMPLE: Bart parks his car in his parents' garage because he's threatened with having it repossessed. That would be a triple tragedy: he'd lose his ride for as long as it takes to get it back; he'd have to buy it back at auction or reimburse the lender's cost of taking it from him (on top of the original loan, which continues to accrue interest); and the repossession goes on his credit record, where it stays for seven and a half years. Bart's parents definitely want to prevent that from happening. They pay off the car loan in full, and Bart has to make payments to them, at the same rate of interest, but without the threat of repo if he's late with a payment occasionally.

Changing a loan to a gift

It's best to decide in advance whether you're going to be repaid or not. Don't pretend it's a loan unless you genuinely plan to make the youth pay you back when he's able. Of course, you *will* have the option of reviewing that decision when the time comes— deciding to make a gift by canceling the debt—but if you lead the young person to expect that in advance, you're undermining the value of loaning it rather than giving it.

183

EXAMPLE: Alicia, the poet mentioned above, is now gainfully employed, but not gainfully enough to buy a car less than ten years old. Her parents give her their four-year-old car, and celebrate her new job by writing off the balance of her debt to them. (This is not enabling; it's giving her a boost.)

MISTAKE: Rick loaned his daughter $4,000 toward a car purchase. He "secretly" intends, when and if she finishes repaying him, to congratulate her for her responsibility and give her back all those payments. The problem is that he's hinted as much; so Libby pretty much expects she'll get that money back. She doesn't feel the cost of the car.

WORSE: Rick changes his mind when the time comes, deciding to keep the repayment after all (perhaps because he thinks she's made frivolous purchases while taking her time about paying him; or because he now needs the money).

BETTER: If you *know* you won't enforce the loan, don't pretend it's a loan. It's a gift. Otherwise, treat it as a real loan with precise terms, part of your Deal. Whatever the time period and payback terms are, put them in writing and enforce them. Give your youth the satisfaction of demonstrating responsibility and financial independence. After she's paid you back, you'll have plenty of opportunities to make gifts in the future.

EXAMPLE: Patrick needs $8,000 to relocate from Massachusetts to Texas, where he has a good job prospect. There are moving costs, security deposit, initial rent and living expenses until his paychecks start. He and his mother estimate that it might be a year before he can start paying her back, and then another sixteen months at $500 a month.

Two years and four months later, Patrick has repaid the debt to his mother. She says, "I'm impressed, though not surprised, by the way you kept our Deal. The fact is, I don't need this money, and you can put it to good use. Please accept it now as a gift."

I think that's a good move if Mom doesn't need the money, provided it comes as a surprise. If Patrick had expected it, and she'd later decided, for some reason, not to give the money back to him, it would feel like a betrayal of unspoken expectations. That wouldn't be good for their relationship.

The *worst* way to handle a loan is to leave it ambiguous: "Pay me back when you can." If Suzy never feels she can afford to repay it, you'll call the money a gift—but when and if she reaches some unspecified level of solvency, you might demand payment? Who'll be the judge of when she can afford to pay you? Will it depend on how much you approve of her lifestyle when the time comes?

Some parents jerk their kids around with money, the promise of money, or the threat of withholding money. Don't.

What kind of parent would charge his own child interest?

Some parents worry that putting their kids in debt to them seems ungenerous. They'd rather be Santa Claus dropping down the chimney than Scrooge banging on the door. I don't think that's the way to look at it. The question—grant or loan?—shouldn't be "How generous do you feel?" but "What's actually best for the kid?" If you're helping them become financially responsible, and you're doing so by replacing an onerous, usurious debt with one on generous terms, why should you feel guilty about that?

Another question is this: If the point of a parental loan is to reduce the payment burden for a child, why charge any interest at all? Often, there isn't any reason to do so—as in the example of Patrick, above. In some cases, though, it might be worthwhile to create an incentive for the young person to pay it back (besides their sense of honor).

> EXAMPLE: Molly's parents feel she sometimes views them as an eternal well of funds. They're about to loan her the amount of her credit card balance in order to relieve her of the onerous rate and, more importantly, to let her decide how much she can afford to repay in any month. However, they want her to be

realistic about two facts: their money was growing, for their own retirement, when they dipped into it to help her; and in the real world we do have to pay for the use of capital. So they set the interest at about the rate their bank would pay a savings account, 2.4 percent. Since they could actually have earned twice that rate in a fixed term certificate of deposit, this is generous on their part. In their hearts, they'd rather not have charged their daughter interest. But they remind each other that 2.4 percent is an almost insignificant rate, the purpose of which is education, not usury.

How much interest? Amounts that are easy multiples of twelve (1.2, 2.4, 3.6, or 4.8 percent) make it easy to add monthly interest without a calculator. For example, if the balance last month was $4,230 and the rate is 1.2 percent (0.1 percent per month), the amount to add to the balance this month is $4.23. At 2.4 percent per year, the monthly interest would be twice that, or $8.46; and so on.

Don't I have to report interest income to the I.R.S.? Can my child deduct it as interest expense? No comment. (Nothing in this book should be construed as legal advice.)

What's the Deal?

Whenever your Deal includes a loan of significant money—the down payment on a home, for example—write out and sign a formal note specifying the terms: beginning date, payment expectations, interest rate if any, and what happens if one of you dies before it's been paid off. This latter, though unpleasant to consider, is important if you have more than one child. The sidebar shows a sample note drafted and signed by parents helping a thirty-year-old daughter buy a house. They simply tucked it with their wills, as a precaution against sibling misunderstanding and conflict in the unlikely event of something happening to them in the near future.

A signed note

August 1, 2007

To ourselves and our Executor:

This letter records the fact that John and Mary Smith are lending Molly Smith $75,000.00 at an interest rate of 2.4 percent per year, compounded monthly, beginning Sept. 1, 2006.

All parties understand that Molly may not be able to repay this loan for some time. We'll record all payments made, on the back of this letter; interest will accumulate on the unpaid portion for as long as Molly requires.

In the event that both John and Mary die while the note is still unpaid, we agree that the remainder of this note shall be settled with the parents' estate in a way that is fair to all heirs.

(Signed and dated by John, Mary, and Molly)

"What have you learned?"

There are silver linings on the clouds hanging over your "ass deep in debt" son or daughter: namely, the wonderful opportunities they now have for learning about personal finance. One part of the opportunity is to learn from looking back, without shame, at how this happened to them. After all, if they made some mistakes, millions of others—no, hundreds of millions—have made the same mistakes. Consumer debt in the United States alone now tops two *trillion* dollars (million million). Our President told us, on at least one historic occasion, that going out and shopping is a patriotic act.

Seriously, take the time as you go over your youth's bank and debt balances, to explore with them where the problem began, and what they'll do if they find themselves at a similar point in the future. As Joline Godfrey notes,

> "Perhaps the greatest gift you can give your kids is the opportunity to take risks and make mistakes. And when the

mistakes show up, the operational question is not what did you do wrong? but what have you learned?"[45]

But that's only the beginning. Now that they're in this process of working themselves out of debt, your coaching and that of others should make them more sophisticated about consumer finance and household money management than their peers who haven't been in this situation. This is a good thing, as each small piece of learning along the way contributes to self-esteem (especially when you acknowledge their learning).

Be realistic

Conveying an optimistic attitude is important as you make your learner realistic about how serious this problem is. It won't be easy to fix it. It may take years, during which they have to work two jobs, cannot borrow more money for any purpose at all, and must do without many material comforts that some of their friends are beginning to accumulate. That's a big dose of medicine to swallow. It requires confidence, as we've said before: "I can do this. It will be worth it. I'm good."

If part of the solution involves their working an additional job or shift, you might encourage them to have at least one source of employment that pays on the spot, or at least every week. As Nick said in Chapter VI, freelance work is stressful and irregular (especially hard for those with ADD), but it's even more so when the freelancer has no money cushion and is trying to get out of debt. They need to be able to count on at least a certain amount of cash coming into the coffers regularly.

Nick on "free work"

I don't know why, but friends often ask me to do what they consider a little favor, which I consider work. It might be just a piece of Flash for their website, or design an album cover, or edit their band's music video. Of course they say "I'll pay

---

45   Joline Godfrey, *Raising Financially Fit Kids*. Ten Speed Press, 2003, p. 129.

you," but they're looking for a ridiculously low price. Maybe there's something about what I do, as well as other crafts like photography or furniture making, that people think you're really doing it for fun. They feel they're offering you a showcase for your talent, which will supposedly lead to lots of work at your normal rate.

But they weren't the problem. I was the problem. You wouldn't believe the number of times I agreed to do stuff that would wind up taking me many hours. I was underestimating the time for my paying jobs, too, but for some strange reason my estimates of how long the free jobs would take were even further off! Even after I had all the work I could handle, I was either flattered by those requests or I just wanted to be a nice guy. Or I'd convince myself this was an opportunity to do something creative, some new challenge. I'd talk myself into believing it would be good for me to do it. I had a backlog of those unfinished projects adding to my stress and, when eventually I felt guilty about keeping them waiting, I would actually put one of those promises ahead of my paying clients.

Finally, Dad had a t-shirt made up, "Friends Don't Let Friends Do Free Work." He sent three of them to me and my roommates, who had the same problem. I can't say it made a difference, but I do enjoy wearing the shirt.

Debts to other family and friends: not your problem?

I noted in the previous chapter that money *owed to* your child by one of his friends is not a matter you want to get involved with, or count on when calculating his financial situation. However, I wouldn't dismiss the importance of any *money he owes* to one of his peers, even though that creditor has no legal recourse.

The severer consequences of ignoring legal debts (eviction, loss of phone, repo man) dictate that he should pay commercial creditors before the $300 he agreed to pay an ex-roommate who left him a couch. You probably wouldn't feel enough urgency to loan your kid money so he can honor that promise, whereas you might well do so when he can't make his rent, Internet, or car payment. Nonetheless, you can respect his desire to honor his word, though you don't honor it for him. You probably learned long ago that negative attitudes toward your children's friends or acquaintances only harm their trust and respect for you. So leave that couch debt on his list, while you recommend other priorities.

So much for general parenting principles. Now let's discuss some specific kinds of onerous debt and their cures.

Debt to financial institutions: Paying off the credit card(s)

I heard a radio advisor tell a young woman not to start paying off her $4,000 credit card balance until she had $1,000 in savings. It's not that simple at all! She would lose at least 15 percent of her money, every year she kept it in a savings account instead of applying it to her debt.

What the radio expert may have meant was that she should keep some savings in case of emergency: if she lost her job, for example, and couldn't pay the rent. But in that case, she could fall back on the credit card; why pay the high price now, if it may never be necessary? The expert didn't ask the caller how secure her salary was, or what resources she might be able to draw on in an emergency. If she were your daughter, perhaps you would be that safety net; in which case, you'd advise her to pay every dollar she can spare, to get out of that high-interest loan. In a genuine emergency, she could turn to you, but right now the critical situation she should be worried about is that credit card balance that's costing her $600 to $1,000 a year.

As I've explained, the so-called credit history your youth acquires by making minimum payments is not worth one dollar, compared to the long-term risk upon her of the compounding, usurious debt and penalties.

If your son or daughter is having trouble making minimum payments on a card, then receives a bonus check for some reason, they shouldn't apply every dollar of it to the card balance, because (unless they can pay off the whole balance) they'll still owe a minimum payment next month. Nonetheless, I would apply the lion's share of any extra money they get their hands on to reduce that credit card debt.

> EXAMPLE: Dahlia owes almost $6,000 on two credit cards. When she moves back to her parents' house, she gets an $800 security deposit back, and no longer has to pay rent from her paycheck, so she suddenly finds herself with an extra $1,500 in the bank.
>
> MISTAKE: She pays all of it to the lender with the higher interest rate. She uses her next paycheck to pay her phone bill, car loan, health club, with barely enough left over to go out with her friends. Three weeks later, Dahlia has minimum payments due on both credit cards. If only she hadn't paid quite so much on the credit card all at once.
>
> BETTER: She pays down the balance on the higher-rate credit card by $1,200, putting the remaining $300 (equal to four months' minimum payments) in a savings account so that sudden unemployment, or a medical expense, won't force a missed payment.

Getting debts reduced

You can't turn on commercial radio or TV these days without hearing ads that promise to get your debts reduced, as if by magic. Most of what they try to imply is misleading, at best. But it's only *mostly* false. There are also reputable counselors who may be able to help, and in some cases they can actually reduce the amount of certain debts. Your job as a parent is, first, to help your distressed youth stay out of the hands of charlatans whose goal is to exploit his or her situation for their own gain; and second, to be a partner in learning about and working through the possibilities.

In researching this topic, we found several good books. The fuller treatment in *Managing Debt for Dummies*[46] is thorough and clear on what to look for and watch out for before engaging with any debt reduction service. I'll only touch on the parental considerations, and some financial factors that many of us in our generation never had to learn about, which now come up for our children because they can't pay their debts.

This situation is a great example of how your child's trust in you is priceless, for both of you. Imagine a youth who gets in trouble with debt, hears an ad for "debt settlement" help, and contracts with an office whose only purpose is to make money off his plight. Two months later, they've done nothing to help him, he's paid them a fee, and his debts are worse.

Your kid, in contrast, comes to you first, and you help her find a non-profit credit counseling agency (which runs very few, if any, radio ads), and you also work with her yourself using the systems we presented in Chapters II, VII, and VIII. Thus she avoids the circling sharks and vultures.

Why did that good thing happen? It happened because your child trusted you with her embarrassing situation and knew you wouldn't shame her or be punitive. As I said in Chapter I, trust between the generations has to work both ways.

Debt consolidation: pros and cons

The phrase "consolidate debts" should be a red flag, especially in mass media advertising. This is a lender who wants to take your debts away from other lenders, package them in a way that may be more manageable for you but is still a high interest, long term debt. Think of it as chasing the wolf a little further from your door, at a price. They're in this business for the same reason the

---

46   John Ventura and Mary Reed, *Managing Debt for Dummies*. Wiley Publishing, 2007.

Find a certified agency

The United States Trustee certifies those agencies that are approved for the counseling that the law requires before people can file for bankruptcy. *Managing Debt for Dummies* suggests that such certification is also the best credential to look for in any credit counselor. "We think it's safe to assume that the certified agencies are reputable. To find a certified credit counseling agency in your state, go to www.usdoj.gov/ust and click on 'Credit Counseling and Debtor Education.'"

—*Managing Debt for Dummies.* Wiley Publishing, 2007

---

original lenders were: because people with credit problems are subject to interest rates that are extremely profitable to lenders. (This explains why junk email subject lines like "be debt free" rival the number of sex enhancement offers.)

Having said that, though, there are two circumstances in which consolidating loans from multiple creditors can actually save money. One is if the debts were incurred when interest rates were higher than currently. If your daughter is paying double digit rates on one or more loans, and interest rates have come down so that a *significantly* lower rate is available, the consolidator may indeed be offering value. The other circumstance is if she has improved her credit record or accumulated some assets that could be used to secure a better loan. In either of those situations, it may be worth listening to what a loan consolidation company has to offer. But if all they're really doing is pushing your debt into the future (consolidating in the sense that you only have one bill to pay, for a longer time), that's no help. It's only going to help if it reduces *both* the amount and number of monthly payments. Nothing short of a significantly lower interest rate does that.

What is a credit counselor?

No one who's in the money-lending business is a credit counselor. There are agencies, some non-profit but also some legitimate consulting businesses, that provide help for a reasonable fee. The key is that they don't have a conflict of interest, whereas the consolidator (or "debt settler") merely wants to take the place of your current creditors.

As long as you and your young person are careful to ask questions about exactly what the credit counseling agency will charge and what they will do for you, you can find such agencies in the Yellow Pages under "credit counseling." (If either of you works for a large company, its human resources department might have a list to refer you to, or your credit union might offer such counseling.)

Beyond the word "nonprofit" in an agency's description, ask for a copy of its letter from the I.R.S. approving its nonprofit status. It's a one page document, and if they don't readily present it on request, go elsewhere. You also want to know whether they're licensed in your state. Get a written contract detailing their services, timeline, and charges, before paying any fee.

The counselor offers more detailed and personalized advice than what we're summarizing in this chapter. For example, she looks at all the youth's bills and explains which ones to pay first. And she suggests that a particular creditor might be willing to negotiate a reduction in the amount you owe. Why would the creditor do that? In order to reduce the expense of having to pursue collection on a debt your youth can't afford to pay, and the risk that they never will be able to collect.

The counselor will look at the youth's monthly income versus expenses (Chaps VII and VIII) and calculate what he or she can reasonably afford to pay every month. The goal is to pay that lower amount without being penalized in the form of a higher interest rate, as a credit card issuer would do. Then they'll either call creditors on the debtor's behalf—if that's part of what you've contracted for—or coach the debtor in how to do so. Before talking to a creditor, it's important for the youth to think about which of the following solutions would be best for that particular debt, and understand why the creditor might agree to them:

- Lower his monthly payment, at least temporarily. The creditor benefits by reducing their risk of his defaulting on the loan.

- Let him make interest-only payments for awhile. This, too, reduces their risk that he'll default.

- Let him move the past due amount to the end of the loan period, since he's unable to pay it now. This is good for the youth who fell behind because of temporary unemployment or an extraordinary expense, but can now resume paying at the original rate. Like both of the above options, this gives the creditor the same rate of return as the original loan did.

- Even if they don't move the balance due, they might waive the penalties; they would rather give that up than risk having to write off the debt entirely.

- Finally, best of all for the youth is to get them to lower the interest rate. Why would they do that? To prevent your finding a consolidator or other competing lender who's willing (especially if interest rates have generally fallen) to lend him the money at a better rate. Do the math: if auto loans are available now at 8 percent, and he's paying 12 percent, the lender is better off lowering his rate than losing him as a borrower.

Medical bills

If the crisis is about overdue medical bills, there's a pretty good possibility that you or a credit counselor can help the youth get some of them reduced once the hospital or physician's office is made aware of her nearly destitute situation. Why? The kindness of their hearts? No. Since she genuinely can't afford to pay them in full, the medical corporation would be forced either to pay the cost of collection or sell the debt at a discount to a collection agent. They should be happy to learn that your daughter is willing to pay the whole amount on a more manageable schedule; or to pay an agreed, reduced amount now..

Child support

Child support obligations may be reducible by mutual agreement, for example, if your son has lost his job. It's also an area where you may want to help meet his obligations, for your grandchildren's sake. If a change in the decreed agreement is proposed, don't leave it to an oral agreement or a handshake; consult a lawyer and formalize any change, to prevent misunderstandings or later disputes.

Repaying student loans

In researching this topic, I was amazed to learn how many different kinds of federal, state, and private educational loans exist, each with different repayment requirements, which change every year or so. Many of them have been sold or absorbed by other companies, with the result that anyone who hasn't kept up their original payment schedule may now have a huge task just in finding out who to talk to, before they can renegotiate the terms and get out of trouble. If you or your young adult has this problem, you need a whole book on that subject.[47]

I'll limit myself to some general points that apply regardless of whether your loan was from the federal government, a private lender, or a state program.

- Don't mess around with these folks, because they don't mess around. Congress has given the Department of Education, and all private lenders as well, tremendous powers to collect from student loan defaulters by garnishing wages or salary, intercepting tax refund checks, or preventing re-enrollment for further education. If the bill goes to a collection company, they automatically add at least 25 percent to the balance due—then there's interest on that.
- Bankruptcy is worse than a bad option for dealing with this problem: it's no option at all. In almost all cases, bankruptcy doesn't eliminate the responsibility for educational loan debts.

---

47   Robin Leonard, *Take Control of Your Student Loan Debt.* 2d edition. Nolo.com, 2000. I also recommend *Money Troubles: Legal Strategies to Cope with Debts*, and *Credit Repair* by the same author and publisher.

- If you or your youth have already fallen behind, don't stick your head in the sand and hope the lenders won't catch up with you. Robin Leonard's book, referenced above, gives detailed advice about how to take the initiative and get hold of them before they get hold of you. The good news is that in many cases they're required to give you alternate payment plans—for example, smaller payments over a longer term, or a graduated plan where the payments increase as your income rises—and you can change the plan year by year, if necessary.

Demonstrating that one is unemployed or in a low-paying job, or in a public service job, may qualify the borrower for a big reduction in monthly payments. However, remember that they do this by stretching the term out. Changing from a ten-year payment plan to one over twenty-five years may make those monthly payments significantly lower, but the total amount paid after twenty-five years will be twice as much as you'd have paid under the ten-year plan. The same is true if you go to a company that consolidates loans, as explained above. The inducement may be a somewhat lower rate, and a significantly lower payment, but at the cost of a much longer period and more money paid to them. (There is no free lunch.) The only good deal is if you can get the *rate* lowered by consolidation and can then pay it off quickly.

Your child's original student loan was probably an example of wise borrowing when originally taken on. It was an investment, which has unfortunately become a burden. As a parent, therefore, you're not enabling a debt addiction if you replace the onerous debt with a personal, low-interest loan from you. (Unless the student loan is only part of a larger, more troublesome picture.) If the debt is a substantial sum, as it well may be after years of higher education, there's a chance the young person might not be able to repay it in full during your lifetime. To avoid issues of perceived unfairness among your children, and so as not to impose payments on your debtor child that his or her income may not allow, consider lending against the inheritance. All you do is pay the loan off for him, get the student to sign a note (with very low or no interest), and attach that note to your wills and trust documents, as illustrated in a home loan example earlier in this chapter.

Bankruptcy

Only a small proportion of young people who get in trouble with credit will actually file for bankruptcy, because their parents will bail most of them out. Still, the laws against drowning are becoming more severe even as the credit industry lures more and more weak swimmers into deep water.

In 2005, Congress passed the first change in the bankruptcy law in twenty-seven years. Authors Dick Morris and Eileen McGann discuss this in their muckraking book, *Outrage*:

> A more cold-blooded piece of legislation would be hard to envision. Credit card companies, the beneficiaries of the bill, posted a profit of $30 billion in 2004, charging exorbitantly high interest rates, peddling credit cards to teens like drug pushers, and charging loan shark-like excessive penalties for even slightly late payments. To augment their profits, the revised bankruptcy law holds debtors in almost permanent bondage to their debts, making a mockery of the very purpose of the bankruptcy statute in the first place. [48]

The 2005 law closed the Chapter 7 "clean slate" route and forced credit card debtors whose income is above the median into the more draconian Chapter 13. A Chapter 13 judge can grant no more than a 20 percent reduction in debts.

> Rather than cure insolvency, Chapter 13 simply perpetuates it. Most people find it impossible to make the required payments over a five-year period, so about 75 percent of Chapter 13 bankruptcies fail. Then, with the debt unforgiven, the hounding by creditors resumes—but this time the debtor has no surcease

---

48   Dick Morris and Eileen McGann, *Outrage*. New York: HarperCollins, 2007, p. 239

Bankrupt: chilling statistics

"The people who consistently rank in the worst financial trouble are united by one surprising characteristic. They are parents with children at home. Having a child is now the single best predictor that a household will end up in financial collapse.

"Our study showed that married couples with children are more than twice as likely to file for bankruptcy as their childless counterparts. A divorced woman raising a youngster is nearly three times more likely to file for bankruptcy than her single friend who has no children. ...

"Bankruptcy has become deeply entrenched in American life. In 2003, more men and women will file for bankruptcy than will graduate from college. ... The number of car repossessions has doubled in just five years. Home mortgage foreclosures have more than tripled in less than twenty-five years. Families with children are now more likely than anyone else to lose the roof over their heads."

—report of the 2001 Consumer Bankruptcy Project funded by Harvard and New York University and the Ford Foundation

---

or shelter until two more years have passed, after which the debtor can refile for bankruptcy and begin the same dismal process all over again.

For most people, Chapter 13 means a life of indebtedness with no relief. One mistake, one serious illness, one lapse into carelessness or irresponsibility, one job loss, and you're serving a life sentence of debt.[49]

It's for those reasons that I believe parents who are in a position to do so should make personal loans to adult children, as long as those children are basically responsible in the present, only crippled by excessive debt from the past.

---

49   Morris and McGann, cited above.

The bottom line

We've discussed many ways you can help young adults fight their way back from serious debt:

- When it doesn't conflict with the goal of teaching them to meet their obligations, you can bail them out of part or all of their debt with a gift.

- You can lend them money at a significantly lower rate of interest, or no interest, and with less draconian repayment terms.

- Whether an outright grant or a loan, your Deal can specify that they won't borrow any more, from a credit card or any other source.

- You can help them slash their spending to the bone. (Remember that if you think they need help with banking and bill paying, your Deal can insist they involve you in that.)

- Your Deal can insist that they take on additional work, more shifts, or change to a lucrative job.

- You can make sure they know the difference between a "debt consolidator" and a trustworthy, not-for-profit credit counselor.

- You can encourage them to be realistic about how long a process this may be.

- You can help them crystallize the lessons their dilemma taught them.

- You can celebrate every positive step, distinguishing your child from the millions who only let their problems get worse through denial and inaction.

XI. Risk Management

What kinds of insurance are important for young adults who are struggling just to pay their living expenses? Should you insist they pay the premiums, for example, on auto or health insurance?

It wouldn't be unusual if the young adult whose solvency you're concerned about had a history, as a child, of losing things, breaking toys (often in the name of creativity), taking risks without weighing possible consequences, and ignoring your nagging about security in general.

In middle school, she lost her wallet, two cell phones, and a Discman.

As a new driver, late at night, he pulled off a country road into a marshy field—don't ask why. You had to go get the car towed out the next day.

As a college freshman, her laptop disappeared from her dorm room. ("Trust me, I do lock the door!")

Some people just have bad luck. Other people are instinctively more security conscious and careful. For both kinds of people, there is insurance.

The good news is, now that you've stopped nagging and become your kid's trusted coach, you can teach the essentials about health, automobile, and property insurance. Call it "risk management" because that sounds more grown-up and intriguing than "did you put your bike in the shed," "why weren't you more careful," and "what the hell were you thinking?"

Whether your nest-leaving kids need to be covered by their own health plan or yours, or by vehicle insurance or a homeowner's, renter's, or other property coverage, is for you to advise them about. This chapter is merely about the concepts that everyone who is considering such protection needs to understand. Chances are, your youth wouldn't pass a quiz on those concepts. Yet they are essential knowledge for anyone to

- engage in discussion with you or an insurance agent about what coverage to purchase;
- fulfill conditions in the contract to maintain the coverage; and
- know how to go through the needed steps in documenting and applying for reimbursement, if needed.

To that end, in sections on the principal kinds of insurance, I'll offer some explanatory language you can use to get the basics across without putting a young person to sleep, as well as quizzes you can require them to pass as part of your Deal.

First, though, let's talk about risk management more broadly than just the problem of buying insurance. It's about a developmental change we want to see in them, having to do with caution, due diligence, and that "T" word again: trust.

Be less trustful

When young people say "Trust me," it's a plea for a better world, in which they *and everybody else* would be trustworthy. They tend to apply the Golden Rule, trusting others as much as they would like to be trusted themselves. So one of the tasks of parenthood, unfortunately, is teaching a child to be less trustful.

I've already discussed this in connection with the marketers of credit cards, and other predatory lenders, where we need to teach our youth that "nice people don't ask you to keep taking on debt." I want to suggest that the lesson needs to be broader than that. Hopefully, we train them to be skeptical of all advertising, of rumors, of the news media, and also of their peers.

`Nick: slow learning`

`Another lesson I learned might be obvious to you, but I only learned about 25 percent of it each time it's happened to me. There was that time the kid ran off with all our cash from the party` in Chicago, but it took a few other hard training exercises for this lesson to sink in. One time, a guy offered me the chance to design the whole look for a new brand of hair products: packaging, print ads, and website. Two weeks of work. Then I found out he had no money. "Get in line." I wound up suing him in small claims court and got a judgment against him, by which time he had left the state. I never got a penny. And I realized that I hadn't had any reason to trust him in the first place. As I looked back, I'd sort of thought he was a bullshit artist from the start.

Many times, I've said to myself, "This doesn't feel right, but I'll boldly ignore that aspect of it because, on the positive side, it would be a good opportunity." Many times, I should have trusted my first, cautious reaction.

It's all very well to take the bad with the good, but you don't necessarily have to *look* for the bad in order to get the good. No, I don't regret going through all those disasters, because that's who I am, but … I've been through enough of them.

Nowadays, if I see the red flag, that there's a chance this client may be broke or might not pay me for months, I get a down payment in advance. If they have a problem with that, or if they want it ridiculously cheap or on an unrealistic deadline, I say "This is definitely the best I can do, so maybe I'm not the best hire for you."

Of course, you've been preaching this all their lives: "Don't believe everything you hear," and so forth. But that's no longer enough. Late adolescence and the twenties are years of growing sophistication. The young adult is developing a skeptical and inquiring mind. He or she realizes that most claims are a mixture of truth and confusion. Advertisements that appeal to us aren't evil, they're an invitation to learn about products we may want to buy. We investigate them by asking further questions, comparing competing brands, reading independent reviews (and questioning their independence), looking into such things as warranties and privacy guarantees, and by reading fine print before we sign.

Such inquiry processes are part of what it means to be a responsible consumer. They're simply due diligence, an important part of risk management.

Unfortunately, inadequate risk assessment is a problem for many individuals with "Attention Money Disorder" (Chapter VI). Dr. Craig Venter led the team that identified the complete sequence of DNA in the human genome. Like many entrepreneurs, he had school problems in the 1950s which, today, would likely be diagnosed as ADD. His autobiography[50] tells how the value of his discoveries to the pharmaceutical industry made him a rich man. But he also attributes the loss of untold millions to the fact that he repeatedly entered joint ventures of one kind or another, in which he optimistically trusted others to share his goals. If he respected someone's talents, even when his wife or colleagues warned him that he was being taken advantage of, he went ahead, assuming he could make the relationship work. Reading that reminded me of some of my clients, and of Nick.

Warnings about risk can have the opposite effect to what a cautious parent, trustee, or other mentor intends. If one sets oneself up as the shrewd voice of distrust and accuses the youth of being foolish and vulnerable, both parties may perpetuate that unrealistic division of roles. The elder's excessive distrust may enable the youth's naïveté. Recently I saw a mother who held her toddler on a leash—not around his neck, of course, but attached to a harness so she could stop him from running away. He kept dashing headlong toward the street, and was safely restrained each time. Instead of learning that his fleeing was a fruitless waste of energy, he seemed to have reached the opposite conclusion: it was a good, safe game. Similarly, parents who can't take off that harness, so to speak, with older children, teens, and young adults, can unintentionally provide an excuse for the latter to dismiss

---

50   Craig Venter, *A Life Decoded.* Viking Penguin, 2007.

their cautions. Don't let yourself fall into the trap of enabling your child's naïve trust by your own prudence and distrust. Your stance should be that he or she is just as smart as you are. You stand *together* on the side of prudence, financial security and safety. Those become matters of joint inquiry and discussion.

Coaching the youth to be knowledgeable about the topic of insurance happens to be something you can insist upon as part of your Deal, if you deem it important in your youth's current situation. Even if you use that leverage to teach about prudence in only one area, the payoff to his or her development is likely to spill over into other types of competence.

Risk management begins at home

In their early teens, you may have had occasion to teach them about what is and is not covered by your homeowner's policy. As they go off to college or to life in an apartment, they need to think about what's at risk from fire, theft, accidental loss. Is it worth buying some insurance? It's nice when you can maintain coverage for them on your policy—talk with your agent, for example, about the computer and other valuables in Johnny's dorm room—but sooner or later they need to consider the responsibility of protecting things as part of their cost of owning them. Just as car insurance is part of the cost of having a car, renter's insurance—or alternatively, accepting the calculated risk of losing one's valuables—is part of the cost of living on your own.

Two other kinds of insurance warrant in-depth discussion and coaching with young people: health and auto. Our concern in this book, of course, is limited to the role you can and should play, as parent or other helping adult, in the youth's ability to acquire the protection needed in each case.

Your role in the two kinds of insurance is similar, in many ways. But it's different in one important way: I recommend shifting the cost of vehicle insurance onto the young person, sooner rather than later; while for health insurance I've found, with my own as well as clients' kids, that it's less important who pays. No kid was ever "spoiled" by having parents provide his or her medical safety net.

Understanding health insurance

As a supposedly advanced society, it's appalling that more than fifty million Americans have no health insurance.[51] And many of us who do have so-called health insurance really only have medical catastrophe insurance, because we have to pay the first $1,000 or $2,500 or $5,000 per person each year, before the insurer takes over.

Nonetheless, I think some parents of young adults worry too much when the latter aren't covered. When Nick and his sisters were small, they thought if anyone in a moving car didn't have their seat belt buckled, the car would crash. (We encouraged this belief.) Similarly, some parents act as if the lack of medical insurance were a disaster waiting to happen. Of course, it's foolish not to protect oneself from those major hospital expenses, rare as they are, when one can. But it isn't cause for panic. I wouldn't advise a young person to take a job that pays poorly and won't lead anywhere, merely to get group health insurance.

I say this only to get you to consider the whole picture objectively when thinking about how to protect your impecunious child from medical disaster. One option, if he doesn't have a job with a health plan, is to help him get an individual plan with a high deductible. If necessary, you pay the premium, deductible, and/or the co-pays so he has no excuse not to go to the doctor as needed. As long as you make sure he's part of the shopping and choosing process, this extended parental care is unlikely to reduce his effort to become self-supporting.

---

51   States vary widely, from about 8 percent of adults uninsured in Minnesota to 31 percent in Texas. Robert Wood Johnson Foundation, *Characteristics of the Uninsured: A View from the States.* May, 2005.

Some resources on health insurance

www.ahia.net, the Association of Health Insurance Advisors, to find an independent health insurance agent in your area.

www.ambest.com, the clearinghouse A.M. Best, which rates insurance companies.

www.canadapharmacy.com, a site for buying prescription drugs from Canada. Compare with www.costco.com and other discount US pharmacies.

www.familiesusa.org, a nonprofit health-care advocacy group.

www.racinereport.com, an interesting forum for people who are uninsured or underinsured.

Fred Brock, *Health Care on Less Than You Think: The New York Times Guide to Getting Affordable Coverage*. Times Books, 2006.

Susan Sered and Rushika Fernandopulle, *Uninsured in America: Life and Death in the Land of Opportunity*. University of California Press, 2005.

I've seen two kinds of situations, however, that are worth questioning.

EXAMPLE: One case is where young people are kidding themselves about being "self supporting." Sheila graduated from art school three years ago. Her mime troupe works the parks and street festivals, making barely enough for the three of them to eat and live in a one-bedroom apartment. Her parents pay for a medical insurance plan, all the co-payments and deductibles, and also dental care. She recently needed new contact lenses, which also fell in the "health" category. They wouldn't want Sheila to go without that care, yet they wonder: are we enabling her denial? Making it too easy for her to avoid facing the necessity of supporting herself? That's a question only they can answer. Perhaps the answer depends upon whether this phase in her life is leading somewhere, or is a dead end that she's in denial about.

EXAMPLE: The second case is more clear cut. Geoff and Rachel made the decision to pay for medical insurance for their son, for their own peace of mind. They pay a fairly high premium on this individual plan in order to keep the deductible low. Nate is responsible for any out of pocket costs; they simply keep the policy in force with $200 monthly payments. What's the problem?

MISTAKE: The problem is they keep reminding him about it. "You wouldn't be able to make the rent on your place if we weren't paying for your health insurance," and similar messages, undermine Nate's pride in the growth he has accomplished. As I've said about other gifts, if you decide to give it, give it constructively. When you think your son or daughter can handle taking on that additional responsibility, bring up the question and negotiate a date for transferring it to them. In the meantime, don't bring it up. You should be congratulating them about what they're doing for themselves, not putting them down for being partly dependent.

Key concepts to make sure they know[52]

Whether they are able to obtain a policy themselves or you pay for it, don't relieve them of the responsibility to know how the coverage works. What is a premium? Co-pay? Deductible? What is the relationship between premium and deductible? (To be knowledgeable enough to shop for a health, auto, theft, or fire insurance policy, one has to understand why premium and deductible are inversely related.)

If the cost of a doctor's visit or clinical treatment is less than one's deductible, is there any reason to go to a physician or hospital that belongs to your plan's network? (Yes. The network's contract with them limits what they can charge for services.)

If one leaves a job through which she had health insurance, is she stuck without protection? (No, but this situation calls for an immediate education about choices to be made before signing off with the employer.)

---

52   An online quiz on this topic is among those on www.EarnTrust.net (accessible without opening an account).

What is a pre-existing condition, and can you do anything to stop it from being excluded by your insurer? (Often, you can. Don't try to hide it; ask the agent before signing.)

Understanding vehicle insurance

Although states require vehicle owners to purchase insurance, they don't require us to pass a quiz on the important concepts— *deductible, liability, comprehensive*, and so forth—that one needs to know when purchasing, and filing claims for, insurance. Most important is the significant tradeoff, as with health insurance, between deductibles and premiums.

You may have picked up the various terms and principles haphazardly, as I did over the years, and unless you're in the insurance business, your own understanding may be sketchy. But as parents of young people who've had difficulty staying on top of their financial obligations, we can make sure they know what they need to know. If they're buying a policy, they have choices to make, based on an accurate understanding of the options. If they're driving a car or truck that we ourselves own and insure, we need them to know what is and is not covered, and what to do in the event of an accident or theft. Because we're actively coaching them with a purpose now, the informal way we presented this information when they turned sixteen is no longer enough. In your Deal, you can insist the learner demonstrate knowledge of these basics.

Coaching a young person about car insurance as well as car loans is a golden opportunity to go over key financial concepts at a "teachable moment" when you have the learner's attention: risk assessment; legal accountability; contractual obligations; collateral; interest; and healthy skepticism about money-saving deals.

To make the most of this opportunity, you might have a look at EarnTrust's material on understanding auto insurance[53]. It

---

53   The interactive tutorial page and quiz at http://www.EarnTrust.net/ advice/insurance is free.

begins with a few explanatory paragraphs aimed at young adults, followed by a quiz you can ask your learner to take. A passing score is 100 percent, but it's "open book." After checking their answers, they can retake the quiz until they've got it right.

Frankly, when pulling the material together for the website, I discovered holes in my own understanding of these terms. So I suggest you go through the exercise yourself, before trying to present it to your kid!

Assuming you have passed or could pass a quiz on the basic concepts, I'll discuss some choices you and your youth need to consider when discussing the purchase of a car.

Can I afford to buy a car? Can I afford not to?

Risk management in relation to buying a car includes more than just the question of insurance. *Driving,* itself, obviously entails risk. *Spending* several thousand dollars on the car is a risk, to one who's living month to month. With that cash spent on a down payment, how will she pay her rent if she loses her job? The car *loan* is a commitment to the additional risk of losing everything one has spent on the car, as well as one's credit rating. We discussed those problems in earlier chapters. (Also see the section on Scenarios in the Appendix, "Using EarnTrust.net™.") We assume, since you're reading this book, you're actively involved in a youth's money concerns and might even make an explicit Deal to help her acquire a car. You'll discuss the full list of costs: purchase; interest on a loan, if required; registration; fuel; routine maintenance; unforeseen repairs; parking; and finally, insurance. Those costs may be balanced by some savings: time on public transportation; taxi fares, or depending on others for rides to school or work.

Annual fuel and maintenance estimates are available online for every automobile or truck model and year.[54] You can also get close estimates, from competing companies, of the insurance cost for the specific car whose purchase you're considering.

---

54   http://www.edmunds.com/apps/cto/CTOintroController

About 15 percent of the cost of vehicle insurance goes to the agent, which is why shopping for it online from the big national firms will often save money. But while shopping for the best rates, I would explain to the youth that companies differ as much in their reputations for how quickly and fairly they service claims in the event of an accident, as they do in rates. Judging by their TV ads, they are all saints in the claims department; but the Internet enables you to compare their reputations as well as their rates.

Doing that research together is just one more step in transforming your relationship from Adult-Child to Adult-Adult.

Questions to discuss with your insurance agent

Is it better for the youth's car to be owned in his or her name, or in yours? The insurance will almost certainly cost less for a second or third car on your policy. On the other hand, would your insurance company disallow claims if the cars are based for long periods in different states or neighborhoods?

Another consideration is that this car may not need the same coverage your own car does. Collision coverage doesn't make much sense if a car is already banged up.

The key, as always, is to see that young adults are informed and involved in these decisions. You can't teach accountability and responsibility by making their risk management decisions for them.

The bottom line

Consumers Union found that the average U.S. household files one claim on their auto insurance every ten years, for about $600. Over that period of time, they have paid an average of $9,000 in premiums. One obvious conclusion is that it's better to be an insurance company than a customer. But we buy insurance in hopes of *not* needing it. We know we'll be out of pocket if we don't file any big claims. It's the relatively unlikely, but potentially catastrophic risk that makes the purchase worthwhile. This is a lesson about risk management in general, which I would not assume your youth knows.

XII. Taxes and Deductions

What young people need to know about income tax falls into two categories. Those with steady employers need to understand what all the deductions are for that reduce their paychecks, and what to do with those numbers on their pay stubs. The self-employed, from whose taxable income nothing has been withheld, have the challenging task of setting money aside, and they may have to pay estimated tax every quarter.

Let's hope the day comes when our children have a huge income tax obligation. Right now, however, they're probably in a low tax bracket. The dollars paid in taxes aren't overwhelming. More commonly, their problems are record-keeping, filing, and remembering what they owe and when they have to come up with it.

Monthly bills are difficult enough, but at least they're on a schedule and they arrive in the mail. In contrast, our tax deadlines are less regular, don't necessarily come with reminders, and we have to prepare considerably in advance to meet them. Annual income taxes are a much bigger hassle than just writing a check.

In this short chapter, I'll make three points. First, even youths whose employers withhold tax, Social Security, and Medicare need to understand the pay stub that comes attached to their checks. What are all those deductions about?

Second, if they have self-employment income (like Nick's freelance fees, for example) they need to set some of that aside, as we suggested in Chapter VII, for the day when the tax man cometh. The neighbor used to pay your daughter in cash for baby-sitting. Don't ask, don't tell. But the club where she works as a life guard will report its payments to the I.R.S. and send her a 1099 form—six months later. After she spent all the money.

Lastly, they should know what happens to those who don't file and pay taxes on time.

Basic tax concepts

Shown below is a typical pay stub for a regular employee. At $8.90 an hour, plus overtime and commissions, Hope multiplies nine dollars times forty hours and thinks, "I make at least $360 a week." If she expects to see that number (or $1,440 a month) in a cash flow projection such as we worked with in Chapter VII, her actual bank deposits will be a rude surprise. This is one reason to go through a pay stub with her and explain the deductions.

Sample Pay Stub

Pete's Tropical Fish
Evanston, IL

Hope C. Kaye

FEIN: xxx-xx-xxxx

period: March 8, 2008 - March 21, 2008

Gross pay	rate	qty	current	YTD
Hourly employee	8.90	80	712.00	4,806.00
Overtime	13.35	6.5	86.78	585.73
Commission	3.50%	1,732.86	60.65	409.39
Gross TOTAL			859.43	5,801.12

Deductions from gross				
Health insurance contribution	50%		73.00	492.75
Dental insurance contribution	50%		9.30	62.78
Deductions TOTAL			82.30	555.53

Taxes withheld				
Federal withholding	15.00%		128.91	870.17
Soc. Sec. employee	6.00%		51.57	348.07
Medicare employee	1.40%		12.03	81.22
Illinois withholding	--		0.00	0.00
Taxes TOTAL			192.51	1,299.45

Gross pay			859.43	5,801.12
Deductions from gross			-82.30	-555.53
Taxes withheld			-192.51	-1,299.45
NET PAY			**$584.61**	**$3,946.14**

You know what all those numbers mean. Don't assume your youth does.[55] In particular, I would show them that they're taking home less than 65 percent of what they "make". However, that doesn't mean they're losing the other 35 percent. Hope's pay stub shows that her $82.30 deduction bought her health and dental insurance; her employer contributes an equal amount. As we said in Chapter XI, she should be aware of how the costs and benefits of this insurance compare with what she might have bought as an unemployed or self-employed person. Also, if she were to cut back to, say, half time with this employer, how would the various benefits change? And what happens when this job ends?

Her Social Security and Medicare payments are essentially retirement insurance, for which the employer pays an equal amount by federal law. Like the health benefit, those are life expenses no one would be subsidizing if she were self-employed. The employer also pays an additional premium equal to about 1 percent of Hope's earnings, for state disability insurance. Add all those insurance and retirement contributions to her take-home check, and they exceed the amount of tax withheld. In one way or another, she has actually received (though not deposited in her own bank) *more* than her gross pay.

Finally, estimated federal taxes of 15 percent have been withheld—that is, prepaid for her. Someone should have explained how they arrived at that number, based on her tax bracket and the fact that Hope has no dependents other than herself.

Her state revenue department doesn't require withholding, because the amount of tax she'll owe in Illinois is so small, at her income level.

The self-employed case
The best thing about Hope's situation is that she probably won't have to come up with any additional tax payments when she files on April 15 of the following year. Salary and wages

---

55   An online quiz on this topic is among those on www.EarnTrust.net (accessible without opening an account).

("W-2 income") are subject to withholding. Freelancers like her brother, on the other hand, have the extra challenge of setting aside a portion of what they receive, for taxes. They may also be required to make quarterly estimated tax payments. We suggested a method to do so, in Chapter VII.

On the bright side, the self-employed have more opportunities to deduct certain expenses as costs of doing business, on Schedule C of the I.R.S. Form 1040. But that's a mixed blessing, as they need help organizing the system of records that will yield those numbers when tax preparation time comes.

`Nick: a fate worse than taxes.`

I had made some estimated deposits for two quarters last year, but when April came around I found I still owed something like $2,700. I didn't have it, but fortunately filed on time so there was no penalty charge. The interest charge for not paying when I filed was only 5 percent per year, but I found out the penalty for filing late would have been 5 percent for every month I was late, up to 25 percent of the amount I owed—in addition to the interest!

What if I'm late in filing or paying my income tax?

Remember what Nick called his "Blissful Ignorance Disorder"? Trust me, he would have let the April 15 deadline sail blissfully past. Luckily for him, his mother assured that his 1040 was filed, even when he couldn't pay the tax amount due. Thus he only owed the I.R.S. that amount plus a 5 percent annual rate of interest. (A heck of a good deal, in these times.) Make sure your learner knows that the penalty is stiff for late filing (unless one files the simple form for an extension), while the interest is reasonable on the lateness of the payment itself.

We're talking here, of course, only about U.S. federal income tax. The state in which he or she files may be more, or less, forgiving than Uncle Sam is.

The bottom line

It's helpful to provide mentoring and free accounting services in the first few years when your adult children are learning to do their taxes. However, the emphasis should be their learning from you, rather than depending on you to take care of the whole job.

Tax preparation, like health insurance, is something we can do for our kids for a few years in the stage when they're getting their heads above water, without enabling any unrealistic behavior on their part. However, if you do their taxes or have them done, make sure to go over the tax form with them line by line, with explanations, before they sign it. It's a great opportunity for them to learn how their financial life is affected by tax laws, and how it can be improved by tax planning.

Those who are so fortunate as to have unearned (investment) income need additional education. The next chapter covers that topic briefly.

XIII. Trust Funds and Partnerships

> *The kinds of coaching we've been advocating could be provided by a trustee (who may or may not be the learner's parent), by another family member, or a paid mentor. A trustee has legal control of certain assets for the benefit of a young person, and therefore has all the more reason to promote the beneficiary's financial knowledge and cash flow management. Distribution terms written in the trust document itself provide guidance and authority for the Deal between trustee and beneficiary.*

Do your children currently get distributions from a trust? Are they named beneficiaries of a trust that will take effect if you die before they reach a certain age? Are you a trustee, or likely to become one, for any young person? (If you answered no to all of those, you can skip this chapter.) If so, this is an important chapter for several reasons:

- We'll discuss how to avoid "trust dependency."
- We'll explain how the trust document itself supports making and enforcing your Deal.
- We'll contrast the role of trustee with that of a parent (though you might have both roles).

An abundance of money doesn't do anything to relieve the aggravation and emotional turmoil arising from irresponsibility or lack of financial skills among the young. Of course, you won't lie awake some nights in fear that your children may starve or be denied medical treatment. On the other hand, they have more expensive opportunities to screw up. Thus they require more education, to manage those opportunities.

Trust: the homonym

The word *trust* in "trust fund" has a very different meaning from that in "trust me." It literally means that wealth was entrusted to someone *other* than the descendant it's intended to benefit.

A legal trust is a structure for conveying property so as to restrict its access or uses. In our society, the most frequent reason an owner of significant assets puts them in trust is that our tax laws offer benefits for doing so: ways to avoid inheritance taxes and gift taxes. Those are not our concern here, except to say that my colleagues and I see many cases where trusts that were created only for tax purposes, or to make wealth last through three or more generations, have also created family conflict, resentments, or passivity on the part of the beneficiaries.

As either a grantor (legal term for the person who puts his or her assets into a trust) or as a trustee (the person who releases funds only for certain purposes, under certain restrictions), or both, you have a mission far more important than saving taxes. Your mission is to help the beneficiary learn to use money responsibly, preserve his or her inherited assets, and (maybe) continue to grow them.

The age fallacy

Trusts for the benefit of young adults mainly involve *not trusting* them to have control of an inheritance. The legal language goes something like this: "Until my Beneficiary's (child's) __th birthday, my Trustee may distribute money as needed for said Beneficiary's health, education, and maintenance. After his/her __th birthday, the Trust shall terminate and the Trustee shall pass its assets to the Beneficiary." In layman's terms: kid, you don't get the dough until a certain age, unless this Trustee person decides to dole bits of it out to you before then, within limits.

Provisions like that reflect the original purpose for which trusts were invented centuries ago, which had nothing to do with taxes:

Clarifying a trust's message

Because a trust document restricts the beneficiaries' power to control family assets, it often conveys a message that the grantor lacked confidence in their abilities. Yet one of its purposes is just the opposite: to allow time for them to develop their abilities before taking on the responsibilities of wealth.

Your first task as a grantor, therefore, should be to think through your reasons for not making an outright grant to your children. Then be sure all the terms of your trust are consistent with your motives and hopes.

Next, write a personal letter to the beneficiaries, with the assumption that you won't be around when the time comes to explain your decision to protect family assets from taxes and creditors and assure a financial safety net for the future. You might remind them of your family values, or those of the original wealth creator. Finally, note that, far from being unworthy of your trust, you have confidence in the thoughtfulness and responsibility with which they will grow to be capable stewards of their family's good fortune.

—Sara Hamilton, Founder and CEO, Family Office Exchange

to preserve substantial assets for their intended beneficiaries, and to limit the purposes for which a beneficiary can spend them while young.

However, the mere passage of years provides no assurance that young people will *ever* be prepared to manage substantial investments or other kinds of assets on their own. On the contrary, having a trustee pay bills, negotiate leases or major purchases, and make major investment decisions without consultation may cheat an adult beneficiary of the financial education he or she will eventually need. In recent years, financial institutions and trustee advisors have come to agree that one of a trustee's most important functions is raising the beneficiaries' sophistication about money. We're talking about sophistication that goes beyond the basic household management skills this book is concerned with, to include such topics as wealth preservation, investment strategies, finance, and how investment income is taxed. It would also include topics relevant to their particular family's activities, such as philanthropic giving, land stewardship, partnership income, or corporate governance.

In the sidebar on the previous page, Sara Hamilton, one of the leaders in getting that message out, discusses what may be the most important element in educating future wealth owners.

Wealthy families are able to provide as much education as their children want, and to launch them into adulthood free of debt. Not only their children, but often grandchildren and later generations. That is a wonderful gift, yet it's not enough. (See Chapter IV.) I agree with Sara and others who work with those families—lawyers, trust officers, financial managers, philanthropic consultants, even their property managers and pilots and nannies—that wealthy families need to give as much attention to building their human and intellectual capital for the future as they give to keeping and growing their financial wealth.

What is *human capital*? It's a term we advisors use for the sum of what a family possesses in the form of talents, personal character, and family relationships. *Intellectual capital* is the combined knowledge all its members have gained through formal and informal education, work experience, and their participation in community life.[56]

> MISTAKE: Clients of mine were three brothers who had just received a windfall—tens of millions of dollars—from their father's sale of his third generation company. Their grandfather had put the stock in trust for his heirs before they were born, but now that they were all in their thirties, they were free to draw out as much of the after-tax proceeds of the sale as they wanted.
>
> The trustee was the head of their father's financial office, who offered to set up independent accounts for each of them

---

56   I've argued that the best index of any family's success is the caliber of human and intellectual capital they've been able to attract through marriage. Kenneth Kaye, *The Dynamics of Family Business*. iUniverse, 2005.

within the family's portfolio of investments. But the two older brothers, both of whom had been living on trust distributions, were eager to get their hands on their money.

Chet had been living beyond his distributions, in fact, carrying high balances on multiple credit cards. Now he was able to pay them off, buy a resort home, a new sailboat, and commission an architect-designed city house. He had several million left over; not enough, however, to generate the income his new lifestyle required. Within three years, he had to choose between losing the house or the boat.

The second brother, Bill, was single and extremely frugal. "I know how much stockbrokers charge," he told me. "I've got a friend who's showing me how to trade online." He did modestly well for the first two years, more or less matching the overall market's gains; then saw his fortune shrink by nearly half within a period of three months.

BETTER: Their youngest brother, Allen, had dropped out of college ten years earlier to start his own business, which was beginning to be successful. He left most of the windfall in his trust, invested a fraction of it in his business, and made no change in his lifestyle. Allen met quarterly with his trustee and investment managers. He told me those meetings were "my business school."

Trust dependency syndrome

Even amid Nick's most painful and aggravating struggles, he and I never lost sight of the most important purpose of our relationship: to get him standing on his own feet. Neither of us was interested in having me help him in ways that kept him dependent on my support longer than necessary for him to grow in earning capacity and self-sufficiency.

You may have heard trust beneficiaries referred to in terms like "trust babies" or "wealth addicts." Assuming the speakers aren't merely jealous, they're voicing a valid concern. All those nice protections and services built into the trustee relationship can deprive a young person of the psychological advantages of learning to manage a modest amount of money, with professional advisors. Brothers Chet and Bill in the example above were examples. No one had insisted they get a financial education during those years when they were dependent on trustees' distributions..

In my profession, I do see some Chets and Bills as well as some who develop passivity, doubts about their entitlement (as I described in Chapter IV), and self-esteem problems. However, I don't see those effects as the inevitable result of growing up wealthy. Nor are they intrinsic to trust funds or to the trustee/ beneficiary relationship. It depends how the trustee treats that relationship. If he or she allows beneficiaries to remain financially ignorant and immature, that surely can work against the goal of building self-sufficiency. Like young children who have to ask for things, they continue to depend on an authority's willingness to release a trickle of funds from the reservoir:

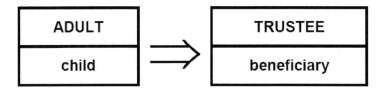

A small number of beneficiaries do, unfortunately, make a career of their dependency. Asking their trustees for more money to burn through can become a game, or a torture.

That isn't really common, however. Most beneficiaries I've known were wise enough and mature enough to live within the means provided by their trustee's interpretation of the distribution conditions. Almost none tried to manipulate their trustees for more, more, more. So I'm less concerned about their having been "spoiled" than about those who haven't been sufficiently trained, in early adulthood—*compelled* to learn, if necessary— about the nature of their trust assets and all that's involved in the stewardship of wealth.

Responsibilities of a trustee

1. To be guided by the grantor's purposes in creating the trust.
2. Within the provisions of the trust, to act entirely for the beneficiaries' long term benefit.
3. To increase beneficiaries' financial awareness and see that they get effective financial education.
4. To meet at least annually with each beneficiary in order to renew their understanding of the trust and to learn in depth about their personal situations, so as to serve their needs better.
5. To advise them about their responsibilities as beneficiaries, and how well they are or aren't meeting those responsibilities.
6. To implement the trust's policies and procedures regarding investment and acceptable risk.
7. To maintain excellent professional advisors in the fields of investment, tax, and law.

—Based on James E. Hughes, Jr. Family Wealth: Keeping It in the Family. New York: Bloomberg Press, 2004.

Joint responsibilities of trustees and beneficiaries

In short, a trustee's responsibilities include education, not merely control over the purse (see box). Fortunately, the fact that you do control the purse gives you great leverage in assessing the beneficiary's educational maturity to handle wealth. Among other things, you have the authority to insist that a youth who has been irresponsible with money get mentoring along the lines we've described in earlier chapters.

"Leverage"? "Insist on mentoring"? Doesn't that sound like what we've been saying since Chapter II? It turns out that a trust is really a legal authorization for, and spells out distribution rules for, a Deal. Viewing it as a Deal makes it easier to remember that the beneficiary is an adult, with each side respecting the other's role.

So, if you happen to be their parent as well as trustee, you have all the more reason to make it clear which hat you're wearing at a particular time. The parent hat counts most when you're praising and when you're explaining your worries, while the trustee hat is often more effective when drawing the line on financial support. It also helps you get past at least some of the emotional residue from that beloved child's long history of making you crazy.

Use the trust document. Every beneficiary aged eighteen or older should have a copy of his trust. Together, read how it defines your duties as trustee, and let those legal duties confer the authority for your Deal.

> EXAMPLE: I mentioned Pete, a wealthy heir, in Chapter II. The section of his trust from his grandfather that dealt with distributions included the phrase "support and maintenance in reasonable comfort, medical care (including, but not limited to, dental and psychiatric care), and education (including, but not limited to, college, postgraduate, professional, or vocational training)." On the next page is the Deal his mother, the trustee, made with Pete.
>
> "Reasonable comfort" gave the trustee permission, though no obligation, to fund the purchase of a home and match Pete's earned income. Although her hopes and concerns as a mother surely guided her choice to encourage more education and give him an incentive to earn money, she took the emotional history out of their negotiation by putting on her trustee hat.
>
> Notice that she merely *encouraged* Pete to earn money for himself. The terms of the trust didn't allow the trustee to insist on that, strictly speaking. However, the incentive she offered, matching every dollar he earned with another dollar from his trust may have been an effective supplement to her maternal powers of persuasion.

Trustee Mother will:	Pete will:	Completed when:	Goal:
match earned income, pay tuition if needed, buy home if desired, mentor Pete, explain Trust terms, authorize accountant for tax matters	live within means, pay own bills, maintain secrecy about Trust assets	12 months without money issues	Pete allowed option to use family office for bill paying eventually, more liberal distributions

An increasingly accepted view of the trustee-beneficiary relationship is one of *mutual* responsibilities: in effect, the trust is no longer just a contract among the grantor, the state, and a trustee. It entails reciprocal responsibilities between trustee and beneficiary, even if (or especially if) the latter has a history of carelessness with money.

Making distributions

Let's assume that the young person you're concerned about has money in trust and is lucky enough to have a conscientious trustee (you) who thinks carefully about (a) the purposes for which distributions are allowed, (b) individual beneficiaries' best interests, and (c) the long term interests of the whole group of

---

Responsibilities of a beneficiary

1. To gain a clear understanding of the grantor's purposes in creating and maintaining the trust.
2. To understand the trustee's proper role and responsibilities.
3. To understand the basics of investment asset allocation and its relation to the balance between a trust's mission of preserving wealth and its mission of providing distributions to beneficiaries.
4. To understand the trust's responsibilities to her as a current beneficiary as well as to contingent or future beneficiaries.
5. To meet at least annually with her trustee in order to renew her understanding of the trust and inform the trustee about her personal situation and needs.
6. To seek evidence that the trustee is properly representing all beneficiaries, and communicate her view of the trustee's performance.
7. To become educated sufficiently about financial accounting to be able to ask intelligent questions about the trust's policies and procedures regarding investment and acceptable risk.
8. To know by what formulas the trust compensates her trustee and other professional advisors for their services, and what each of their compensations amount to.

—Based on James E. Hughes, Jr. Family Wealth: Keeping It in the Family. New York: Bloomberg Press, 2004.

---

beneficiaries.[57] As trustee, you constantly balance your duty to provide for them in the present with your duty to protect the assets for the future. Each beneficiary individually might like to receive as much as they can, as soon as they can. However, they

---

57 It may be impossible for an institutional trustee (a bank's trust department as opposed to an individual selected by the grantor) to provide adequate mentoring, because (a) the bank has to run itself as a business, making a profit from its trustee fees, which limits the time it can devote to beneficiaries; and (b) the institutional trustee role is often filled by a young trust officer, a position with frequent turn-over.

all share a financial interest, whether they think so or not, in how well you conserve and build the value of their *retained* assets.

However, that is only true while the assets are still in the trust. Once you've decided to distribute funds for any purpose, the beneficiary isn't accountable to you for those. You were never *his* trustee, you're the trustee of the assets in his trust. The moment some money becomes his money, let him spend it and experience the results. If you want to set preconditions on funding something, you can write a letter containing the word *IF*. Suppose the beneficiary wants to enter a postgraduate program, for example. You could approve the funds for one semester while agreeing to pay the second semester's tuition IF he earns at least a B average in the first semester. You don't really have authority to impose a consequence for poor grades unless you've spelled out something like that in advance.

There's no doubt that values come into play when you're a trustee. The grantor expressed certain values but left you much latitude to interpret them in the light of your own values (which he or she considered when naming you trustee), as well as the times you live in (perhaps far removed from the grantor's) and the particular needs of this beneficiary. The last of those considerations is likely to prove the most important.

For example, although Pete's mother in the example above felt he should experience earning money in a job, other trustees might consider earned income less important than financial education, and the latter may be an equally good source of satisfaction and self-esteem for some beneficiaries. Bringing in money through one's own sweat contributes to self-confidence in many young people, but it isn't the only path. Many people whose life work is of an artistic or charitable nature, or who serve their family interests in administrative ways without "earning" a dime, seem to be quite secure about the worth of what they do. Thus the most important question is what the trustee, today, thinks the beneficiary needs.

Partnership income

Some tax issues requiring specific knowledge arise in connection with capital gains. They can be problematic if you put assets in your son's or daughter's name in a family partnership, which you have been managing. Unlike a trust, which pays the taxes on its investment income, a partnership's gains are taxable to the individual partners.

> EXAMPLE: Your daughter, Erica, is a one-third limited partner in FamPartners, LP. As the managing partner, you're selling one of the partnership assets at a $300,000 profit. That's a taxable capital gain for Erica, of $100,000. No problem, if you distribute the money, which she might like. However, that's not your plan; you sold the appreciated stock in order to buy other investments, not to enlarge her lifestyle. What you'll probably do is distribute just enough from the partnership to cover the taxes.
>
> The partnership books list Erica's share of the gain from the sale as $100,000, of which $15,000 was supposedly distributed to her and $85,000 retained in a "capital account" for reinvestment.
>
> Yet Erica's I.R.S. Form 1040 shows capital gain income of $100,000, with a capital gains tax of $15,000. As managing partner, you distributed the $15,000 to her account, from which a check went to the I.R.S. with the tax filing. So she never got a penny of that $100,000 income she sees on the form.

Assuming you're treating Erica as an adult, you'll have some explaining to do. Why does her 1040 show income many times greater than what she actually earned last year? Where did the money come from, that you're giving her to cover the income tax? And how is it fair that she has to pay tax on it, when you never coughed up the hundred grand?

> MISTAKE: One of my clients had built a portfolio of investments for each of his daughters that was worth nearly $200 million. The women didn't know the value was anywhere

> ### *Maturity guidelines can be written in the trust*
>
> Psychologists Mitchell Baris and Carla Garrity, with estate attorneys Carol and John Warnick, wrote a paper that virtually sums up the whole philosophy of this book. They suggest that the grantor of a trust can require a trustee to measure the beneficiary against specific dimensions of maturity:
>
> "The trustee could also be encouraged to be more liberal in making distributions as a beneficiary demonstrates competence in managing his or her distributions. The trustee could be warned about falling into a pattern of predictable discretionary distributions that might impede a beneficiary's progress towards self-sufficiency and self-advancement. Likewise, the trustee guidelines might suggest that large distributions, other than those needed for the purchase of a home or getting started in a career or business, should be delayed until the beneficiary has made significant progress in a majority or perhaps all of the benchmarks of maturity."
>
> — "Maturity Markers: A New Paradigm for Trust Distribution Models and Gifting Strategies," © Family Firm Institute (www.ffi.org), 2007

near that high. At forty-nine and forty-four years old, all they knew was that Dad had made millions and they were "set for life." He bought their houses and their cars. He paid their taxes, their insurance, their children's school tuitions. (Of course, he kibitzed all their personal purchasing decisions.) One daughter was aware that Dad made those payments using money that was already, somehow, in her name. Her sister thought it was a gift, each time he sent her a check or paid the mortgage. The daughters assumed correctly that most of that fortune would come to them when their parents died, but they felt it would be presumptuous and ungrateful to ask questions about the dollars involved, much less ask why they shouldn't take charge of those assets themselves.

This father wasn't acting within the law. After placing investments in his daughters' names as a tax-avoiding device, he still treated it as his own money. For example, he declined to pay for college for one daughter's stepson; a decision which, legally, should have been entirely hers and her husband's. But my main concern, as a family psychologist rather than a lawyer, was this: having denied his daughters the opportunity to come into his business, he also treated them like perpetual children. They respectfully enabled his keeping them in the dark, allowing his accountants to file their taxes. (Happily, in his late seventies, this man accepted advice and became supportive of their growing financial sophistication.)

Writing a trust?

You may be in the process of, or thinking about, creating a trust for your children's benefit in case you don't live long enough to see them make it through to financial maturity. In many ways, the law dictates how you can protect their assets. But the most important element is under your full control, as a grantor: to appoint the wisest trustee(s) you can, and give them explicit guidelines about how much discretion to use in making distributions from the trust.[58]

How can you, as a grantor, prevent trust dependency syndrome and ensure that when you're not in the picture, your children's or grandchildren's trusts will be vehicles for learning financial responsibility rather than excuses for not doing so?

My colleague Sara Hamilton's firm, Family Office Exchange, works with families around the world who have passed down large fortunes through trusts across several generations (in some cases, for centuries). Sara says one of the greatest challenges of a grantor is finding someone both qualified and appropriate to serve as trustee. "It's a challenge to find someone with the wisdom and strength," she says, "to say 'no' to a beneficiary whose request

---

58   James E. Hughes, Jr. *Family Wealth: Keeping It in the Family*. New York: Bloomberg Press, 2004. Also: James Hughes, *Family: The Compact Among Generations*. Bloomberg Press, 2007; Stuart Lucas, *Wealth*. Wharton School Publishing, 2006; and Charles Collier, *Wealth in Families*. 2d Edition. Harvard University, 2006.

today may not be in the best interest of their later years, when they need greater support. Most family members have no proper training for the role, and asking a relative to serve as trustee can actually damage their family relationship with the beneficiaries."

That problem has spawned an entire industry of professional trustees employed in trust departments of banks or in trust companies. "If you look to personal friends instead," Hamilton says, make sure you find someone wise and thoughtful, but also younger than you. They must bridge the gap between you and your children for the life of a trust, if it's the kind that will terminate at a certain age. And if it's the kind that they will remain beneficiaries of all their lives," [as is often the case in preserving large fortunes for later generations] "it's essential to specify the process by which successor trustees will be chosen long after you are gone."

The bottom line

Whether you are the grantor of a trust, or a trustee for your own children or someone else's children, you need to make clear to all parties that the trust's real purpose is to help beneficiaries become *trustworthy* stewards of their good fortune. Above and beyond whatever its tax advantages may be, it exists because they were not yet ready to be trusted with significant wealth. It is in their interest, as well as in the interest of preserving their family's human and intellectual capital, that they be trained and supervised in handling financial capital.

Therefore, this book's suggestions about written and signed Deals, about mentoring, and about the course of development from childhood dependency to adult mutual trust apply well in situations where the ownership and distribution of funds are restricted by legal documents.

XIV. Other Mentors

Although we mainly addressed the largest group of our readers, concerned parents, most of what we've explored in this book also applies if you're a paid mentor or a friend. Furthermore, the learner you are helping could be of any age, young merely in financial experience. This chapter discusses some differences from the parental relationship. One matter is constant, though: What's your Deal?

Who else might be a learner's mentor? A grandparent, uncle or aunt, an older or younger sibling? An ADD coach? We discussed trustees in Chapter XIII. A family's accountant often makes a good mentor. Any accountant is comfortable working with ledgers, but the best ones are able to teach that comfort to their clients. A valuable mentor could be anyone possessing the basic skills for managing a bank account, bills, and short-term planning; whom the learner trusts or will learn to trust; and who doesn't have a material conflict of interest or a conflicting personal agenda.

If you are in that position, you may find the role easier than it is for many parents. The advantage of detachment—freedom from family baggage—can be considerable.

Yet this, too, is a relationship. It's just a different kind. Whether your background is financial, counseling, pedagogical, or spiritual, think of the coaching as a personal relationship, which you'll strengthen gradually as you build the learner's self-esteem, trust, and belief that you're genuinely there to help rather than control or spy.

On the other hand, as a non-parent mentor, don't fall into the trap of feeling you have to take care of an irresponsible youth's affairs without the appropriate effort on his or her part. It's just as important that the Deal be explicit and enforced between you and the youth as it is when parents mentor their own kids.

EXAMPLE: The CEO of a large company employs a bookkeeper, Doug, to manage her private expenses as well as those of her college-aged daughters. "I give orders all day," she tells Doug. "I don't want to be teaching my kids how to manage their business." Each daughter gets a monthly allowance. Doug's responsibilities include watching their bank accounts and, more importantly, educating them in many of the topics we've discussed in this book.

Daughter Marlys, twenty-two, is taking a year off from college to work in filmmaking. Her allowance eliminates the economic hardship of a minimum-wage freelance production assistant. When not on the road with a film crew, she lives in a modest apartment in Los Angeles. The rent is within her means, yet somehow there are money issues each month: late payment charges on the utility bills, other bills Marlys forgot to send to Doug, or last minute requests for advances on next month's allowance.

MISTAKE: Because Doug prides himself on being a problem solver, he keeps Marlys out of trouble so effectively that she doesn't learn to manage the mundane side of life. She's always too busy to spend the hour it would take, once or twice a month, to meet with Doug or get on the phone and computer and go through it with him.

BETTER: Doug should enforce the Deal. He could say to Mom, "This arrangement isn't helping Marlys grow up. She may need to go in the hole and feel the financial consequences a time or two, to realize the value of making a little effort and focusing on cash flow and planning."

Accountability

You're accountable to whoever's putting up the dough. If you're a trustee, as I explained in the previous chapter, you're accountable to the grantor and the financial interest of *all* the beneficiaries, not just the one you may be mentoring.

Similarly, if a parent pays you to act as mentor, or even if you're doing it as a favor but some money passes to the youth through your control, make sure you have a clear statement, in writing, of *three* agreements: yours with the parent, his or her Deal with the youth, and your Deal with the youth.

EXAMPLE: Doug, the bookkeeper just mentioned, would probably use the form of a memo to record the three agreements that his assignment entails. We're using a table here to show the component parts in each case:

Doug's Job with Mrs. H.:

Mrs. H. responsible for:	Doug responsible for:	Completed when:	Goal:
pays Doug, communicates with Doug and Marlys	monthly reports on Marlys cash flow and reliability	all 3 agree M no longer needs Doug's help	Marlys financial independence and understanding

Mother / Marlys Deal:

Mother responsible for:	Marlys responsible for:	Completed when:	Goal:
contribute $2,700 per month to Marlys's account	live within income plus allowance, no unpaid VISA balances or other debt, work with Doug a minimum of 2x/month	all 3 agree M no longer needs Doug's help	financial independence from Mother

Doug / Marlys Deal:

Doug responsible for:	Marlys responsible for:	Completed when:	Goal:
put monthly allowance in Marlys bank, confer with her semi-monthly	pay bills, keep checking acct records online to go over with Doug	all 3 agree M no longer needs Doug's help	increase Marlys financial under-standing

When you don't control the purse strings

Almost everything in this book so far has assumed that the mentoring Deal includes providing some financial help: a parental gift, a loan, a trust, or non-monetary support such as housing or a vehicle. But there's another whole category of mentors who are *only* mentors: you don't control the purse strings, and you're accountable to no one but the learner who has asked you for coaching. You may be an ADD coach, an executive coach, a counselor, or a friend. I know several people whose brothers and sisters, or even parents, have turned to them for help of this kind. The learner isn't necessarily dependent on the more successful or prudent family member for money. Nor do they need to be desperately in debt to recognize that they're squandering money, missing tax deadlines, failing to keep proper records, or being taken advantage of by others. What if a friend or relative, of any age, turns to you for help in such straits?

You still need a Deal. You're not offering money on your side—the client may even be paying you—but she needs to know what you expect of her in this working relationship, and what she can and cannot expect of you. And you both need a clear focus on the goal: what's the criterion for "graduating" from your tutelage?

EXAMPLE: Gary has definite responsibilities for a substantial part of his support, though still not all. His sister has agreed to take on the role of mentor because the father-son relationship is too strained. Gary pays for his phone, utilities, food, and personal expenses himself. He forwards to his sister the rent, dental, and medical bills their father is still covering (she takes care of the paperwork for health insurance reimbursement), as well as his biweekly pay stubs for tax accounting. Gary is responsible for upkeep and repairs to his material assets: car, electronics, clothing, and so forth. His sister can look at the online bank account and the EarnTrust™ account at any time, but Gary tries to keep those up to date. If there is a discrepancy, they resolve it during their monthly phone session, jointly reconciling the ledger and discussing the key performance graphs.

Sister will:	Gary responsible for:	Completed when:	Goal:
write checks on Dad's account for rent, dental, medical; handle HMO reimbursement, keep tax records	basic expenses, upkeep, maintaining online bank records	he no longer needs family support, and passes Banking, Credit, Tax tutorials in EarnTrust.net	end of sister's oversight

Without knowing more about Gary's limitations or the family circumstances, we have no reason to judge the wisdom of Gary's father's unconditional financial support. Regardless, his sister needed to make her own Deal with Gary clear, for his benefit as well as her own.

The bottom, bottom line

The person you're concerned about is a legal adult, and wants to be treated as an adult. Your opportunity to capture his or her attention and motivation doesn't come from relative size, age, or parental authority. It comes from the fact that you, or someone who engaged you, is subsidizing a person who's in financial distress due to a lack of knowledge, or attention or learning problems, or plain old carelessness—and you're willing to help.

That's the Deal: make it explicit. Negotiate it thoughtfully, write it down, be prepared to follow through. The rest is merely common sense. The result will be a grown-up citizen who enjoys mature, mutually respectful relationships with other adults.

This is the bottom line about the words, "Trust Me." No longer must we pretend that anyone beyond high school is equally entitled to the status of a grown-up, no matter if they haven't taken on grown-up responsibilities with money, no matter whether they're chronically dependent on bail-outs of one kind or another. Nor do we have to nag or patronize them with judgmental advice that undermines their self-confidence. By proving their reliability one step at a time, they can earn our trust in their maturity.

And by helping them, we will have earned theirs.

Appendix: Using *EarnTrust.net*™

Our website, www.EarnTrust.net, built by Brian Begy and his team at Chicago Data Solutions, is a suite of interactive tools for the same concerns and strategies we discussed in this book. How do those tools facilitate the principles we have advocated here, and what do they add to the system we've described?

(For clarity, SMALL CAPS designate specific pages on the website.)

The free tools

Many of the website's features are free. NICK'S ADVICE to his peers, DR. KEN'S ADVICE pages, the SCENARIO displays, TUTORIALS, and QUIZZES are accessible without a subscription. You can use the DEAL form as a guide to clarify and print out the terms of your Deal. The sample ACCOUNT LEDGERS display a hypothetical young adult's earnings and expenses, with which you can experiment to see how buying a car, for example, or changing jobs, or moving will affect one's bottom line over the course of months.

The subscription

If you choose to subscribe, you or the learner can save his or her bank transactions, monthly bills, debts, Deals, and "what if …?" scenarios in a secure database where both of you have immediate online access to them, simultaneously if you wish. In order to apply EarnTrust™ tools to a learner's own financial accounts, one of you opens a monthly subscription and invites the other as learner or as coach. The one who initiates the subscription will be billed on a monthly basis (cancellable at any time).

The table on the following page shows some advantages and disadvantages of different types of personal money management software. EarnTrust's strengths are in the collaboration between learner and coach, the absence of paid advertising disguised as purported "free advice" based on your data, and the way EarnTrust™ extrapolates from past transactions to paint your

	Quicken™ Desktop software	Quicken.com™	EarnTrust.net™	Other websites	Paper & pencil
Cost (2008)	Initial purchase, $35 to $65 plus $9.95/mo for bill-paying feature	$2.99 per month (no bill-paying option)	$17.95 monthly fee	Supported by targeted ads based on users' financial information	Free
Advantages	Extends to investment accounts, other assets, mortgages, etc. Direct links to most banks Compatible with TurboTax software.		Designed for learners aided by a parent or other coach.	Direct links to most banks	Simplest, if learner has only one or two bank accounts
Coach and learner locations	In same room	In same room	Together or separate, different privileges possible	In same room	In same room
Up- and download bank data?	Yes, and bill-paying is an option	Yes (but no bill-paying)	Download only, in current version (check future releases)	Download only, for most accounts	No
Advice for mentor and youth	No	No	Yes—step by step coaching	Targeted ads based on users' financial information	(This book)
Security	Excellent	Excellent	Excellent	(If above is acceptable)	

Two months free

Whether you bought or borrowed this book, if you've read this far, we'd like you and/or your learner to try an EarnTrust™ subscription with their own checking, savings, and debt accounts at no cost for 60 days. Just type this code **iUniverse** in the "Coupon?" box on the signup page.

(Remember, you can browse the tools, advice, and sample accounts for free. Only subscribe if you're ready to start using www.EarnTrust.net with your own financial accounts.)

---

financial picture over future months. It assumes that learners need to base decisions on actual income and expenses to date, rather than a pie-in-the sky budget.

I have organized the following sections in line with the chapters of this book.

"Trust Me"

The learner and the parent or coach log into their subscription with distinct usernames. EarnTrust™ does not store your surnames, addresses, social security, bank account or phone numbers, or any identifying information other than a password for each of you and the first names or nicknames you tell us to substitute for "Learner" and "Coach".

To open subscriptions for more than one learner, just vary your own username, for example BobGsCoach, SueFsCoach, JuansMom, and so forth.

What's the Deal?

Like the system in this book, the EarnTrust™ website relies on the fact that you're offering support (financial and/or mentoring) in exchange for certain behavior on the learner's part. Her commitment might be simply to share her earnings and payments info with you so you can coach her, or to restrict her spending, make loan payments on schedule, achieve particular savings goals—whatever the two of you negotiate. Spell it out, including how you will use the website.

The DEAL page doesn't do anything you couldn't do with pen and paper or email, but EarnTrust™ prompts you to complete this important step and keeps your signed Deal for easy reference. In Chapter II, we mentioned that a Deal is only one step in a process of earning trust. Accordingly, the website will invite you to specify a higher level of trust and freedom as the next step when the current Deal's terms are met, or fall back to more restrictive rules if the current goals aren't achieved.

You will be able to have EarnTrust™ keep track of certain quantitative criteria that might be in your Deal: for example, a passing score on specified quizzes, or a bank balance above a threshold amount for a set period of time, or no increase in credit card balances.

In the Coach's PROFILE, you set privilege levels for each of you on the site: who is allowed to enter and edit bank transactions in the LEDGER, or update the DEBTS LEDGER, or declare your Deal fulfilled.

Money's not Enough

If all you wanted were to keep tabs on the learner's bank account, you could have done that merely by insisting on access to it through his bank's website. The purpose of an EarnTrust™ subscription is to mentor. That means making your support more than financial, and setting conditions without being judgmental. As I said in Chapter IV, even when the problem *seems to be* money, money isn't enough.

Motivate: Parents or coaches provide incentives and make it clear the effort will be worth it. You can use the EarnTrust™ DEAL to keep the incentives at the forefront. But the real motivation is more subtle: the learner is gaining your respect. You need to show this both with explicit praise and implicitly, by speaking as one adult to another. No nagging. No condescending tone. On some pages, Nick or I will add our praise for positive steps.

Teach: EarnTrust™ does a great job of confronting learners with the reality of their situations. It does so through the monthly balances, cash flow graphs, and its PAYMENTS TOOL, as well as Nick's and "Dr. Ken's" frank ADVICE (tutorial) pages. But *too* heavy a dose of reality, wisdom, and advice stops being helpful. You will assess whether the person you're mentoring is ready for more understanding, say, of compound interest; or car insurance or tax planning. You can assign a tutorial and quiz the learner yourself, or ask them to take one of the "open book" QUIZZES, which they can repeat until the program reports their passing score to you. Think in terms of small steps and slowly growing confidence as opposed to cramming.

Support: In many cases you, or the parent or trustee if that isn't you, are helping a youth financially. Whether you provide an allowance or a place to live, or someone else is paying you to coach their son or daughter, that financial support has emotional implications, which can be good or bad. As coach, your availability is supportive, and your positive attitude will be even more so. At the same time, don't let financial support go beyond what's helpful. If an allowance undercuts self-reliance or self-esteem, dependency might become a permanent way of life. Our goal, and yours, is to see learners graduate from their EarnTrust™ joint subscription to self-sufficiency in handling their money.

"Attention Money Disorder"

Unlike a printed page, a web page can hide material so it's not a distraction, then let the user click it open when he needs it. The website takes advantage of this to optimize the learning environment for people with attention or learning difficulties, by expanding and collapsing months and groups of transactions within months. Users can see as much or as little detail as they need at the moment.

The same principle governs pop-up help, the table of DEBTS, TO-DO lists, and individual topics on the HELP page.

The TYPICAL MONTH and PAYMENTS TOOL are especially designed for detail-challenged users who prefer manipulating objects on the screen rather than typing numbers.

Banking – using account ledgers

You can type your transactions into any ACCOUNT LEDGER manually, or import a file from your financial institution in one of several compatible formats. Most people will find it more convenient to use the IMPORT WIZARD. You'll still have to enter manually the future payments or deposits you want to be reminded about, and later confirm them as you import the file of actual transactions from your bank.

You can enter an expected payment or deposit without assigning it to a particular ACCOUNT until its time comes. That's one of the unique advantages of EarnTrust's™ FORECAST LEDGER, discussed below.

Quicken® and its competitors are fine for recording what you did in the past and present: every transaction can be assigned to one of a long list of categories that you need for tax or other historical purposes. But we found them unsatisfactory at extrapolating to the future, especially for a visual thinker like Nick. What does EarnTrust™ do differently?

1. It's for a pair of users, one coaching the other.
2. It's about understanding the learner's existing financial circumstances dynamically, bringing light on what's subject to planned control.
3. It is especially designed for learners with current problems tracking money, meeting obligations, and predicting their cash flow. It's not for those who need to track investment accounts and other classes of assets or financing. Credit card debt is as fancy as EarnTrust™ gets. The site's intended users are looking for clarity and learning. The big picture rises to the forefront.

The designers have balanced your need to see specific trends with the need to keep numbers from overwhelming a learner.

4. It forecasts future cash flow based on the past six months as well as hypothetical SCENARIOS the user can create. Of course, any prediction is only a guess, but EarnTrust™ tries to generate the most accurate cash flow predictions it can, based on the information you've entered. It makes smarter predictions by insisting you distinguish among those three types I suggested in Chapter VII: extraordinary, regular (scheduled), and irregular transactions.

Classifying events

EarnTrust™'s procedure for entering transactions in a bank or credit card ACCOUNT LEDGER requires you to classify each event first according to how it should be used by the forecasting engine (extraordinary=not, regular=repeated on a schedule, irregular=group monthly average). Then it encourages you to assign irregular events further, into the smallest number of categories that you really believe will be useful.

Extraordinary means "this is a unique event, to be ignored for forecasting purposes." As we cautioned in Chapter VII, don't classify an expense as extraordinary unless it's *really* extraordinary. On the income side, it's probably smart to be conservative and count a gift as extraordinary: a windfall, rather than something predictable. But on the expense side, lots of things come along unexpectedly that should not be considered extraordinary. For example, EarnTrust™ does classify the down payment on a car as extraordinary, in the CAR PURCHASE SCENARIO. But what about an $800 transmission job? Although you're unlikely to face another transmission job for years, the irregular category "car maintenance" is hardly extraordinary. Use that, or even just "car" (if you plan to include fuel and insurance in the same group).

Regular (scheduled) means "in addition to this date, repeat the event on a designated schedule." It can be the same date each month, or every other Friday, for example. The program expects the most recent amount to repeat, but you can change it when the time comes. These are deposits or payments the program reminds you to make and to confirm. Expected events don't enter into calculating the *current* balance in an ACCOUNT until they're confirmed. But unless specifically deleted, scheduled bills and other unconfirmed events do affect EarnTrust's prediction of the future net balances.

Irregular means "no specific repetition in the future; instead, assign to [*selected*] group so all transactions with this description produce a forecast for the group as a whole." You can manually enter a future deposit to or payment from a particular ACCOUNT, as a reminder item to be edited, deleted, or confirmed. But the transaction won't affect subsequent forecasts beyond itself, because forecasting is based on actual past behavior.

The Forecast page

This is the screen where you and the learner will get most of your information for planning and what-if purposes: your combined FORECAST LEDGER, across all checking and savings ACCOUNTS, credit cards, and other obligations you list under DEBTS. Unlike all those ACCOUNTS, the FORECAST LEDGER goes eleven months into the future, including extraordinary events you told it to expect, scheduled transactions, and a monthly forecast for each group of irregular transactions (its average over the past six months, or since you created the group if less than six months ago).

SCENARIOS create temporary events or temporarily changed forecasts *only* on the FORECAST page.

More about past versus future events

EarnTrust™ assumes that when you enter or confirm an event with today's date or earlier, this was an *actual* bank deposit or withdrawal. (It didn't necessarily clear the bank yet, but you took the action.) You can always correct it later, if in error; but otherwise it appears in a particular ACCOUNT LEDGER and affects that ACCOUNT's balance on the OVERVIEW and PAYMENTS TOOL pages.

Unless classified as extraordinary, it will also affect predictions on your combined FORECAST LEDGER.

Events entered with *future dates* are always unconfirmed. Those will come up as reminders, for a user to edit, delete, or confirm when the time comes. They appear on the PAYMENTS TOOL described below (ten days in advance of their date), and as expected transactions in the future months displayed on the FORECAST page. If you specified an ACCOUNT (optional for future transactions), you also see them listed at the bottom of that ACCOUNT LEDGER.

Any forecasting program has to use precise rules to extrapolate from historical events to best-guess predictions. You can find explanations of EarnTrust's guesstimating rules as '?' pop-ups on the FORECAST page. But the important generalities to keep in mind are:

- The forecasts improve as you accumulate up to six months' accurate records of actual money in and out.

- Forecasts will be more accurate, meaningful, and useful to the learner, the *fewer* forecast groups he or she uses for irregular transactions. For example, an "entertainment" group will usually forecast more accurately than movies, restaurants, sports events, and parties.

- Forecasting from the past is only your starting place, only as good as the assumption that past behavior will continue. That's why EarnTrust™ has "what-if" SCENARIOS, as well as the ability to enter expected events or adjust the forecasts for irregular groups manually.

A future event on an ACCOUNT LEDGER, the FORECAST page, or the PAYMENTS TOOL (either a monthly reminder, or just a single planned transaction), is displayed in amber. It changes to red when the date has passed, and stays red until a user with confirm privileges clicks its description and edits, deletes, or saves it. (Users with vision peculiarities can select alternate color schemes on their PROFILE.)

Cash or miscellaneous. As Nick said in Chapter VII, "You can get in trouble with cash very fast." Yet it isn't practical to track everything one pays cash for. We suggest assigning all miscellaneous transactions that you don't care to track, and any payments your bank reports that you neglected to record and can no longer identify, to the irregular forecast group "cash". This is the "other stuff" we talked about in Chapter VII.

There are a number of ways you might create an adjustment transaction to bring an ACCOUNT LEDGER's balance in line with what your bank or credit card statement shows. As a default, that adjustment goes in your Cash group, so you can't ignore it entirely. You can go back and reassign "Cash" transactions to other forecast groups, if you choose to do so.

Credit cards. If the learner uses a credit card, store all its charges and payments in a separate ACCOUNT whose balance will normally be negative: a liability against the assets in his or her bank accounts. Since one makes payments against the card balance as a whole rather than for specific items, the allocation of purchases to forecast groups will occur when you import transactions to the credit card ACCOUNT LEDGER. This means that an expense group—for example, one called "gifts"—can appear in a checking ACCOUNT, a savings ACCOUNT, and also in the card ACCOUNT, if different gifts were purchased by writing checks, withdrawing cash from savings, and using plastic. You can click up a pie chart for gifts as a proportion of all purchases from any one ACCOUNT, or from all ACCOUNTS combined (on the TYPICAL MONTH and FORECAST pages). A user who wants to keep track of gifts from distinct individuals would name the forecast groups something like "gifts–Mom" and "gifts—Dad," though for most learners that would go against our advice: keep it simple, student.

The Payments Tool

Nick sketched the idea for this utility while chatting with an acquaintance about what lengths they would go to avoid facing the bill payment chore—even more aversive to them than it is to those of us who consider numbers our friends. How great it would be, they agreed, to use a drag-and-drop tool with blocks on a screen instead of only words and numbers.

You can use the interactive PAYMENTS TOOL to try out alternative moves: which bills to pay immediately, which ones to hold for the next paycheck, how much to pay on the credit card. Using your balances in each ACCOUNT and the list of bills crying to be paid, the program takes you through an interactive, visually compelling version of the exercise we did in Chapter VII. Either or both of you can try moving money in or out of savings, paying or postponing various bills or debts, to find the solution that works best from the points of view of solvency, minimizing credit card interest, or avoiding late payment penalties. Click "Do this," and EarnTrust™ converts the trial action list to reality. Your expected transactions now appear in ACCOUNTS on the appropriate dates and in your FORECAST LEDGER and TO-DO lists, ready for you to confirm the actual bank transactions (only after you've mailed the checks or paid electronically through your bank).

Other graphic displays

What is the best information display mode for your learner? Some people "get it" from a neat LEDGER of numbers; others get more from visual blocks that are sized proportionally, such as bar charts. Still others prefer line graphs displaying trends over time. On many of EarnTrust's pages, you'll find different ways of charting income versus expenses (bar chart), trends over time (line graph), or an income or expense group as a proportion of all income or expenses (pie chart). If your learner responds better to visual displays, point to those rather than the numbers while discussing each month.

The TYPICAL MONTH page displays in all three modes: a list of the dollar values of monthly transactions and the irregular categories; income and expense bar graphs showing the relative sizes of each category within them; and line graphs showing how deposits, payments, and net balance across all ACCOUNTS have fluctuated over the past six months.

The TYPICAL MONTH page and FORECAST page display how the average income and expense categories you've named will affect the learner's cumulative balance over the year ahead. Your learner can then use the SCENARIO WIZARDS to see how major purchases, moves, or job changes will affect his or her solvency.

Choose whichever display seems to be the best teaching tools for your learner, conveying the key messages: is he moving in the right or wrong direction? What should she plan to change?

Debt

Besides credit cards, to whom does the learner owe money? You and who else? The EarnTrust™ DEBTS LEDGER corresponds to the debt table we discussed in Chapter VIII, essentially a monthly self-report. Don't include here any loans that are being paid off (including principal) in monthly installments, because those payments, already shown on the FORECAST page, will discharge the obligation. The DEBTS LEDGER is for debts whose repayment is unscheduled, depending on available resources. Not all loans begin with money going into the bank, and not all repayments come out of a bank account. So you'll need to update this screen manually, as the learner borrows or repays money. Doing so once a month is probably sufficient.

When you enter or update individual loans, the program will ask if there's an interest rate involved. As with credit cards and savings ACCOUNTS, forecasts include approximations of interest accruing, based on the interest rates you most recently recorded. Obviously, the program cannot calculate the exact interest if the rate fluctuates, but we assume an approximation is better than neglecting to take accumulating interest into account.

Advice or Tutorial pages and Scenarios

The tutorial pages on www.EarnTrust.net (no subscription required) are interactive: learners learn by answering questions and posing their own SCENARIOS. On most topics, they can take an online QUIZ and keep trying until they score 100 percent. Some of the topics covered are:

- Financing a major purchase
- Auto insurance: types of coverage
- How does health insurance work?
- What are those deductions on my pay stub?
- What is compound interest?
- Keeping records
- My lease: What am I signing?

One of EarnTrust's best training tools is the SCENARIO, which you can enter from your FORECAST page or from ADVICE pages. Information about buying a car, for example, includes a tutorial on insurance and other topics to think about before choosing a particular vehicle. You can then create a CAR PURCHASE SCENARIO with a name such as "2004 Porsche," where the SCENARIO wizard walks you through questions about price, down payment, miles you expect to drive per month, loan, insurance, and so forth. That SCENARIO becomes a choice on your FORECAST page – toggle it on to see the extraordinary (down payment, sales tax, registration), regular (loan, garage rental, insurance), and irregular forecasts (fuel, maintenance). When the Porsche proves to be unrealistic, toggle it off and try a 1997 Taurus SCENARIO instead.

Other SCENARIOS include JOB CHANGE, HOUSING CHANGE, CREDIT CARD PAYMENT, or a change in any one forecast group (for example, "what if I spent less on clothes?").

Taxes

The system we suggested in Chapter XII to set aside a proportion of any pre-tax earnings received, in a separate savings account, works more simply in EarnTrust™. When you create an income description for the first time, the TRANSACTION WIZARD asks whether these earnings will create a tax obligation. If so, it prompts you for a percentage to use as "estimated tax accrued" in the DEBTS LEDGER.

At that point, whether you actually put the money for taxes in a separate account or not, you have correctly offset a portion of the income deposit (assets) by a liability. In other words, the OVERVIEW page's "Bottom Line" (net balance across accounts) subtracts that obligation from your assets. Don't knock yourself out in calculating the percentage to set aside; I suggest using an arbitrary 15 percent, as the purpose is mainly conceptual rather than to set aside the precise amount.

If the learner does have a savings account, or opens one for this purpose, be sure to create an ACCOUNT LEDGER for it. Then, when money is available after paying bills, use the PAYMENTS TOOL to transfer at least enough into savings to be able to cover the tax obligation when April 15 (or a quarterly estimated payment date, if required) arrives.

Benediction

Whether you open an EarnTrust™ SUBSCRIPTION and use it to track your learner's finances over a period of months, or merely browse its advice pages, tutorials, and quizzes, please leave a note to us there with suggestions to make it even more useful (*feedback@earntrust.net*).

Working on this book together and conceiving of EarnTrust™ have been labors of love for this father and son. More than that, in fact: a profound revelation, a transformative experience, ultimately a confirmation of mutual trust. Nick and I wish nothing less than that for you and your sometimes befuddled, frequently befuddling, always beloved young adult.

Index

C

Made in the USA
Lexington, KY
31 May 2010